KIDS BEDTIME DEEP SLEEP MEDITATIONS 2 IN 1 BUNDLE

Guided Night Time Short Stories and Positive Affirmations To Help Children & Toddlers Fall Into Deep At Night, Relax, And Have Beautiful Dreams

Author: Sleepy Willow

Copyright 2021 – All rights reserved.

The content contained within this book may not be reproduced, duplicated or transmitted without direct written permission from the author or the publisher.

Under no circumstances will any blame or legal responsibility be held against the publisher, or author, for any damages, reparation, or monetary loss due to the information contained within this book. Either directly or indirectly.

Legal Notice:

This book is copyright protected.

This book is only for personal use. You cannot amend, distribute, sell, use, quote or paraphrase any part, or content within this book, without the consent of the author or publisher.

Disclaimer Notice:

Please not the information contained within this document is for educational and entertainment purposes only.

No warranties of any kind are declared or implied. Readers acknowledge that the author is not engaging in the rendering of legal, financial, medical or professional advice.

The content within this book has been derived from various sources. Please consult a licensed professional before attempting any techniques outlined in this book.

By reading this document, the reader agrees that under no circumstances is the author responsible for any losses, direct or indirect, which are incurred as a result of the use of the information contained within this document, including, but not limited to: errors, omissions, or inaccuracies.

TABLE OF CONTENT

Kids Bedtime Sleep Meditations

Introduction 2
Chapter 1 4
    The Ancient Story Book 4
Chapter 2 14
    Enchanted Treehouse 14
Chapter 3 22
    Pirate Adventure 22
Chapter 4 38
    Wishing Waterfall 38
Chapter 5 48
    Ancient Mountains 48
Chapter 6 57
    African Safari Adventure 57
Chapter 7 66
    Magic Crystal Island 66

Chapter 8 73
    Koala Grove 73

Chapter 9 81
    Wolf Guardian 81

Chapter 10 90
    Puppy Kingdom 90

Chapter 11 99
    Owl Spirit 99

Chapter 12 106
    Limiting Belief Buster 106

Conclusion 147

Kids Bedtime Meditations For Sleep

Introduction 151

Chapter 1 153
    Sleepy Space Adventures 153

Chapter 2 176
    Monster And Alien Friends 176

Chapter 3 201
    Private Paradise 201

Chapter 4	227
White Feathered Owl Adventure	227
Chapter 5	242
The Frog And His Magic Drums	242
Chapter 6	250
Sam The Pirate Fish	250
Chapter 7	259
Chakra Meditation	259
Chapter 8	268
Lucid Dreaming Meditation	268
Conclusion	278

KIDS BEDTIME SLEEP MEDITATIONS

Guided Night Time Short Stories And Positive Affirmations To Help Children & Toddlers Fall Asleep At Night, Relax, And Have Beautiful Dreams

Author: Sleepy Willow

Do not listen to this audiobook while driving or operating machinery.

INTRODUCTION

Thank you for listening and choosing *Kids Bedtime Sleep Meditations*.

In this magical and wonderful book, you will be taken on many adventures and listen to wonderful stories that will help you to fall asleep peacefully every night. I hope that you and your children will have hours of fun listening to these stories. Each story in this book will be entertaining and will have small lessons that your child can learn from. You will learn many skills that can help you relax your mind and body, so you have the most amazing sleep every night. Each story contains valuable lessons while relieving stress. Each story will empower you and your children to improve your self-confidence and self-esteem. You will learn how to deal with your emotions better and communicate them more effectively.

Children who experience lots of nightmares might be scared to fall asleep at night and might have a hard time relaxing at night because they are afraid of scary dreams. This book will help you combat and get rid of those fears. Each story will help you feel more relaxed, calm, loved, and completely safe. You have nothing to worry about from now on.

After you have brushed your teeth, combed your hair, and put on nice comfortable pajamas, it's time for you to snuggle down in bed and get ready for sleep. You can now pick any story to help you relax and drift off to an amazing sleep.

Make sure you listen to each story and follow along. Each story has a relaxing meditation to help you get cozy and comfortable for a good night's sleep.

Are you ready to begin your bedtime meditation stories? Choose any story to begin your adventure now!

CHAPTER 1

The Ancient Story Book

Welcome to this part of the book, which is a guided sleep meditation.

This is where you will discover the enchanted and mysterious storybook.

Are you ready for this adventure using your incredible and wonderful imagination?

You will embark a journey to the peaceful ancient forest.

This is where the magical storybook is waiting for you.

If you are now ready to discover this magical and enchanted storybook's secret hiding place, then I want you to close your eyes now.

Make sure your body is comfortable and snug for you to relax deeply.

Remember that only all of the meditation magic happens in that dreamy state of being almost awake and almost asleep.

Now imagine you are at the countryside with your family.
You are staying in a log cabin on the edge of an ancient and wise forest.
Now imagine you are standing outside your cabin in the garden, looking at all of the tall trees.
Imagine how peaceful it is here.
You now quickly feel the fresh earthy air on your face.
You now easily smell the fresh smell of wildflowers and grass.
You hear the happy chirping and singing of birds and the humming bees buzzing along.

The breeze of the wind is so gentle against your skin.
You feel the warmth of sunshine upon your face.
The sunlight is bright and glows all around you.
It is like a glorious force field.
Take some deep breaths in and out.

You are now feeling so relaxed.
You are now feeling so connected to the land and to the healthy and earthy energies of nature.
You start walking past the flower bed and past the vegetable patch.
At the very end of the garden, you push open the wooden gate and close it behind you.

A wave of freedom and excitement washes all over you.
The forest seems to be inviting you to explore it further.
You follow the green grass path that winds through the trees.
The grass feels so soft and fluffy underneath you as you follow this twisting path.
You look around, and you see to your amazement that some of the trees have old and wise faces on their ancient tree trunks.
It looks as if these giant trees are smiling with happiness, wisdom, and making silly faces at you as you walk past them.
You smile back happily at their funny and kind faces as you walk past these trees.

You notice now that the old trees are looking in all different directions with their eyes.
They are pointing the way along the path by looking in different directions.
You allow these ancient wise old trees to guide you as you follow the ways their eyes are pointing.
They are leading you down a winding path deeper and deeper into the forest.
You trust the wisdom of these trees and they are showing you the hidden way.
You wonder what you will discover as you follow the secret way of the trees.

You have now arrived at a massive, gigantic oak tree.
It is the biggest and tallest tree you have ever seen.
It is utterly beautiful and magnificent.
This oak tree is so thick and all of the branches spread upwards and outwards.
Expanding so wide and all the way up to the tip tops of the forests.
The oak tree has the wisest and kindest old face on its trunk.
It kind of reminds you of an old and ancient wizard.
You now notice the trunk is hollow and has a natural space big enough to climb into, but it is really close to the ground.

The massive oak tree smiles down at you, and you sense it is inviting you to explore the inside of the tree.

You are feeling very excited and very curious.
You climb up and into the hollow tree.
Inside it is like a wooden cave.
It looks quite mysterious and surprisingly cozy.
In the middle of the tree is a small table and has a big brown leather book on top of the table.
You now take a closer look.
The cover of the book has lots of pictures of strange and magical creatures.
There are also symbols you do not recognize etched into the book.
The book is painted with what looks like real gold.
The edges of the book looks very old.
It could be from ancient times in history.

You can tell that this book is not modern at all.
It looks like it is handmade by an ancient artist.
You slowly reach your hand out and run your fingers along the pictures and symbols that are so precisely carved into the cover of the book.

The illustrations on the cover are of dragons, unicorns, lions, and every other magical creature you can ever imagine.
With a deep breath, now you decide to open the book.
You open the book and touch the pictures of all the celebrations in the book.
You also look at ancient maps of different and strange lands.
The book is so heavy, and a puff of golden dust glows and sparkles from the book all around you.
Wow, this is amazing.
This gold dust starts to swirl around and dazzle you.
Little spirals of light dance and glow up from the pages.
To your surprise, as you look through this ancient book, you see it contains many myths, fairy tales, and legends told from long ago.
Even some of your favorite stories of all time are in this book, waiting just for you.

The illustrations from this book are some of the most beautiful and unique paintings you have ever seen.
The painting is so detailed.

The writing of the book was handwritten in a lovely script font in black ink.

Now suddenly, the golden magical energy that dazzled you and your whole body now starts to shrink you.

You shrink down and down.

Smaller and smaller.

You are now absolutely tiny!

You are now standing on the pages of the book.

All of these pictures suddenly spring up into 3d all around you.

The pages of the book have come to life.

All of the characters in the book wave, welcome you, and start talking to you.

Wow, this is so amazing!

Now you realize and understand you can be whatever character you want in the story.

You can be the hero of the story and the most important character in the story if you wish.

Wow, this is so much fun.

Any story that you can possibly imagine is right here in this book, waiting just for you.

Whatever fairytale you want or a storyland that is enchanted is waiting for you to explore it.

The storybook will take you there instantly.
You feel so alive and happy.
Wow, this is such an amazing and exciting adventure.
What story do you want to be apart of now?
What character would you love to meet and possibly maybe go on an adventure with?
What character would you like to be?
Spend some time now to just look at the book and just turn the pages.
The magical pages.
You get to pick and enjoy being a character in any story that you wish.
When you hear my voice return, it will then be time for you to dream off into the most happiest and deepest dreams.
Have some fun, and I will be with you again soon.

After you have spent some time having the most wonderful and amazing time turning the ancient book pages and living in the fairy tale storylands, it is now time for you to return back home.
Wave goodbye to all the characters in this magical, enchanting book.
All of the characters now wave back to you, and a sparkle of golden dust shimmers all around you.

You now start to grow bigger and bigger and bigger until you are once again your normal size.
You now close the magical storybook with both of your hands.
You now thank the storybook for the fun adventure.

You wonder who wrote the book, and you wonder who illustrated all of the pictures.
Well, I guess it will forever remain a mystery.
You climb out of the hidden hollow space of the ancient wise old oak tree.
You give the tree a great big hug.
The old wise old face smiles at you with happiness and wisdom.
Now you see that the oak tree's eyes look towards the way back home.
As you walk past the wise, kind trees, their eyes point and lead you in the direction you need to go through the forest.
Their wise old faces lead the way smiling down at you and helping you get back home.

When you arrive back at the log cabin, you climb into your warm and cozy bed.

You feel the warm covers all around you.

You feel so safe, loved, and amazingly happy as you just drift off to sleep deeply now.

You have a sense of fun and freedom that fills your heart as you drift off into the most beautiful dreams. You know in your heart that the enchanted storybook is waiting just for you to return.

The magical enchanted book is always going to be there resting on the little table in the ancient wise old oak tree for you to read and enjoy anytime you wish.

Sweet ancient old enchanted storybook dreams.

29 minutes

CHAPTER 2

Enchanted Treehouse

Now welcome to a dreamy sleep meditation.
This is where you will discover the most fantastic and magnificent tree house hidden deep within an ancient forest.
This special treehouse is waiting just for you.
Now just close your eyes, and let's begin our journey.
Remember the meditation magic can only happen in the sleepy place where you are almost awake and almost asleep.
Now get really comfortable.
Take a big deep breath in and a long breath out.
That's wonderful.
Again take a deep breath in all the way down to your belly and then a calm breath out.

Now your body will keep breathing like this all by itself as your whole body relaxes now.
Your eyes and mouth are now fully relaxed.
Your belly is totally relaxed and free.
Your arms and legs are feeling very heavy now.
Even your hands and feet are relaxing now too.
That's fantastic.
Well done.

Now imagine you are standing in a beautiful forest.
The trees are tall and wise.
These trees also have fairy lanterns and fireflies all hanging around their branches.
The grass feels oh so soft and fluffy underneath your feet.
The moonlight is shining down between the trees making the entire forest glow.
You feel and sense this is a magical and enchanted place.
The starlight sparkles down over you and all-around your body.
You are now shining like a bright star too.
You are feeling so safe, loved, and calm in this forest.

You now notice a path made up of the moonlight shining the way between the trees.
You start to walk along this path now following the silvery moonlight.
It twist, turns, and winds through the forest as it leads you deeper and deeper into the ancient forest.
You walk along a stream of water that is bubbling along.
The silvery moonlight is shining down.
You can see pixies and fairies flying and darting about.
They are dancing on lily pads and on rocks.
They are playing by the babbling brook and maybe even going for a dip and having a swim.
They all smile and wave to you as you walk by them.
This path continues to lead you alongside a crystal clear stream.
You now breathe in and notice the air is so healthy, damp and you can smell the fresh scent of lavender flowers.
The grass is soft and tickles your bare feet very gently.
The moonlit path stops now, and it circles around the oldest tree in the ancient forest.
You look up at this old tree, and is it absolutely so massive.
It also has a tiny door in its trunk.

It has strong branches that have dark green leaves that stretch out into the forest.

A gnome is sitting on a red-spotted mushroom by the doorway of the tree trunk.

The gnome now smiles at you and blows a magic puff of gold dust into the air.

The little door swings open very slowly.

You are now feeling very curious, and you step inside the old tree.

To your amazement, the tree trunk is hollow, warm, and very cozy.

There are soft, warm woven rugs placed on the floor.

There are pictures of stories, legends, and myths carved into the tree walls.

There are mythical and fairytale creatures all carved in and drawn into the wood of the tree.

You realize that anything is possible here.

This is the entrance to your enchanted and magical treehouse.

How would you like to get to the very top of your treehouse?

Well, to your surprise, you notice there are three choices for you to climb up inside the hollow old tree trunk.

You see a magical climbing rope that carries you straight upwards.
There is also a magical and enchanted staircase that goes round and round and creates a wind tunnel.
Or there is an enchanted and magical flying lily pad from the babbling brook.
This lilypad is big enough to stand on and will float you upwards.
Now I want you to make your choice.

Suddenly you are now up at the top of the treehouse!
Imagine this is the most magnificent treehouse you have ever been in and seen.
It is a massive treehouse with lots of rooms inside of it.
It also has different levels and stories for you to explore and play in.
How would you want to decorate each room in the treehouse?
You are allowed to paint them any color you wish.
There are rope ladders everywhere for you to climb upon.
There are also binoculars to look into and across the entire forest all around you.

There is also a telescope to look up and gaze at the planets and stars in space.

You give out a big sigh of happiness.

Wow, it is so wonderful here in this peaceful magical forest at your very own private treehouse.

What else would you like to have in your treehouse? Just use your imagination now, and everything will appear right before you.

You can even invite your friends to come and visit you at your enchanted treehouse.

Which friends would you like to join you now?

Even animals are allowed to come and play with you here.

Which animals would you wish to cuddle and play with in your magical treehouse?

Whatever you wish to do and whatever you want to see is all possible now here in your magical enchanted treehouse.

Now you start climbing through the branches of the old tree.

You just found a bird's nest, some chipmunks and squirrels, and some butterflies that glow in the dark. You also find some other fantastic creatures in this old safe, and wise tree.

You feel so happy now and free.
Keep playing and climbing around.
This is your magnificent treehouse for as long as you wish.
When you hear my voice returns, it will be time to fall deeply asleep.
Have fun now in your treehouse, and I will be with you very soon.

After having so much in your treehouse, you know that now is the time for you to return home.
You wave goodbye to your fantastic forest friends.
What way do you want to travel back down the tree trunk?
Would you like to take the floating lilypad, the spiral staircase, or the magic rope?
Make your choice now.

You now have arrived quickly and safely down back to the floor of the tree.
The door mysteriously opens for you, and you step outside.
The old, kind, and loving gnome smiles at you and blows a magical golden cloud of dust over you again.

You are now starting to feel very very sleepy.
The moonlight shines down and sparkles the soft green grass path.
It is leading you back through the forest.
With every step you take, you feel more and more relaxed.
Sleepier and sleepier.
In your heart, your say thank you to the enchanted forest for this magical adventure.
The ancient forest starts to fade away, and you are now back in your warm and cozy bed.
You snuggle under the covers, and you fall deeply asleep.
You now have pure joy in your heart, and you can now dream fully happy.
This was the most beautiful treehouse in the entire world.
You now smile to yourself as you drift off into a comfortable sleep.
You know that this is your magnificent and magical treehouse waiting for you to return anytime you wish.
Sweet magical treehouse dreams.

(Music

25 Minutes

CHAPTER 3

Pirate Adventure

Now, as your eyes are closed, I hope you enjoy daring and exciting adventures because you are about to have the most amazing and fun journey you can imagine, full of surprises.
It is will beso brilliant it will feel like a dream.
As you close your eyes and listen, you settle into your coziest rest.
Your imagination can begin now to run free.
Explore all the beautiful possibilities of your magical dream coming true.
I wonder if you can believe that incredible legends are really possible.
Perhaps even legends that involve pirates, whales, and lost treasure.

As you just lie on your back, just let your arms and legs and even your belly relax.

You may feel yourself relaxing more and more as you take a deep breath in through your nose.

Let the airflow out.

Good.

Now take another few deep breaths in and out.

As you breathe, you may notice the air sounds just like the relaxing waves of the ocean flowing in and out so easily.

That's excellent.

You're doing great.

You are doing this bedtime meditation brilliantly.

As your eyelids completely relax, they are still gently closed.

Allow this sensation of the relaxing and calming ocean waves to really take over now.

Now start to imagine a big blue ocean wide and free with rolling waves that stretch out as far as the eye can see.

These waves are so relaxing to listen to.

As you really listen in, you think you may even hear the faint sound of a whale song far off in the distance.

All of a sudden, using your imagination, you visualize a pirate ship floating along the big blue happy waves.

As you start to see this ship, a picture is clearly forming in your mind's eye.

You are about to see how impressive this pirate ship really is.

You are now standing on the wooden deck of this incredible pirate ship.

As you look up and around you in amazement, you appreciate how huge it really is.

It is made up of timber like the big pirate ships in stories with an old, tall, and robust mast with large black sails.

At the helm of the boat, there is a brass statue that looks like a mermaid.

The most exciting thing you can hear and see is the flag that is flapping in the breeze.

This flag has a skull and crossbones painted on it.

This is the mighty flag of pirates.

You know that for sure, this is a pirate ship.

Suddenly lots of pirates emerge all around you on the deck of this ship.

You look around, and instead of fearsome and grim-looking pirates, they actually look so friendly and happy.

Instead of having scars on their faces, every one of them has a wide and welcoming grin.

They all look so genuinely happy to see you.

These are peaceful pirates who are welcoming you to their proud pirate ship.

You smile back at them, and you notice the peaceful pirates are all around the same age.

They explain to you that they have lots of fun sailing around the world and looking for long lost treasure.

Their mission is only to seek out treasures that are long forgotten buried in time where no one knows where it is.

The treasures that are buried deep beneath the depths of the deep deep ocean.

You listen to all this, and you immediately think this sounds so much fun.

You start thinking about exciting adventures you might take with them.

You wonder about it now and imagining a peaceful pirate hat on your head.

It is painted with the same symbol of their flag with a mermaid.

How amazing!

The peaceful pirates are officially inviting you to join them on their extraordinary adventures.

You are going on a voyage to find the glorious treasure chests that are said to be in a coral reef under the deep blue waves hidden by the most notorious pirate of them all.

Blackbeard.

Blackbeard was one of the most fearsome pirates who was said to have looted the most bountiful of pirate treasures in all the world.

One of the friendly pirates tells you in a whisper that only a very magical and special whale knows where the sunken mystery treasure is located.

The peaceful pirates have been searching forever for the treasure, but they have not found it yet.

Maybe you can help them find this very magical special whale.

Now you look up and see the beautiful horizon and the orange sun starting to set.

You feel so very satisfied to be here.

You are also starting to feel a little tired.

You just lie back into a hammock, swinging ever so gently on the deck just thinking about all of your happiest thoughts.

Thoughts of how you can help the peaceful pirates finally find this magical whale and Blackbeard's sunken treasure.

As you begin to sway back and forth, you are feeling so calm and relaxed even more.

Just relaxing to the sound of the ocean waves.

Just rocking back and forth in the breeze of the sea.

Just listening to the gentle sounds of the ocean relaxing you to sleep.

Deeper and deeper, you go to sleep.

The rhythm of the waves is lulling you to sleep into the magical land of your dreams.

Sinking Deeper and deeper down, down and further down into your most relaxing state.

You are enjoying this lovely safe, peaceful sinking feeling until you realize that the ship is actually starting to sink.

You jump up and look over the edge.

You see, the ship is now low in the ocean.

The water is about to spill over the edge into the ship.

Then all of a sudden, something incredible and surprising happens.

You are feeling the boat starting to rise up higher and higher.

You are now moving the opposite way, as if the whole pirate ship is being pushed up out of the water by a powerful, strong force pushing the entire ship back up again.
It is now resting easily on top of the safe, calm waves.

The peaceful pirates all let out a cheer as they quickly found and fixed the water leak by pumping all of the seawater out.
Now everyone is feeling relieved again, feeling entirely safe.
You are feeling a little curious as to what or who might have saved this mighty ship.
You and all of the peaceful pirates look together over the side of the boat, looking into the deep blue sea.
Suddenly there is a gush of water that sprays up into the air.
The water gushes so high, going higher than the mast of the ship.

Suddenly an enormous but very friendly face emerges above the breaking waves.

This is the most enormous face with the happiest and biggest smile you have ever seen.
You feel so much warmth and kindness in your heart as you recognize this lovely animal.
This is the biggest mammal on Earth.
He says, hi I'm willy the whale, but you probably know that I am a whale because of my blowhole and my size.
You laugh and nod at Willy the whale's voice.
Even all of your pirate friends laugh too.

You are feeling very brave now, and you step forward to thank Willy for rescuing all of you in the nick of time.
Willy says, no problem, I love helping friendly people out, and the peaceful pirates are always welcome in all of the seven seas.
You also ask Willy if he could possibly help you with something else.
You ask Willy if he knows the secret location of the hidden treasure.
Willy grins the biggest and widest grin showing his big white teeth.
Willy says, follow me to the treasure.

You humans are so funny thinking that things made out of colorful metal and stones are so important. They are actually not that important to me, but it's okay I can help you locate the long-lost treasure chest with my sonar abilities.
They call me Willy the wise whale, and I can show you right now.
Come down and jump onto my back.
Just watch out for my blowhole.
Hold onto a barnacle or two.
You find it very easy to hang on safely.
You step carefully off the ship edge and jump off and onto Willy's huge smooth rubbery back.
It is actually really easy to just hold on tightly as you hang on to some of the bumpy barnacles, which are stuck to Willy's smooth rubbery skin.

You look behind you, and you see all the peaceful pirates wave and cheering for you.
Willy starts swimming, gliding, and takes off.
His strong whale fins cut through the frothy ocean waves.
Willy is the gentle giant of the sea.
He is even bigger up close.
You feel so free, loved, special and strong to have such an amazing and great friend at your side.

You see dolphins swimming alongside you, dipping and diving and squeaking with happiness and joy.

They are gliding along with you between the crashing waves.

Wow, these dolphins are so fun and so cheery and so happy.

They make you laugh so much with their squeaking.

Now something really incredible happens.

Willy is so wise and so kind.

He has such a magical and special type of energy.

Willy now gives you the gift of being able to breathe underwater.

Sit still and hold onto his back.

You both go down underneath the ocean through all of the bubbles.

You are gliding down together, getting deeper and deeper under the waves.

Right here, beneath the ocean, you look out around you and admire all of the ocean life around you.

It is such a spectacular sight to see.

You see schools of strange tropical fish all swimming around.

You see a magnificent octopus swimming by as well.

You even see some electric eels all living and swimming happily about.

What you love the most is the whale song of Willy.
He is singing loving, calming, and happy tunes.

You can now hear other whales singing along and back to Willy even though they sound very far away, but it is so clear for your ears.
It is so soothing and lovely to enjoy the music.
You realize the is the special sonar ability Willy has.
He is such an intelligent creature that is so pure of heart.
Willy is tracking the hidden location of the long-lost treasure for you.
Willy's song is so beautiful and becomes so charmingly pleasant and sings just for you.
Now when you dream of the ocean, it is full of surprises.
Just relax and sleep.
There will be treasure before your eyes.
Wow this is so amazing.
You can tell that Willy just loves to sing his beautiful, loving, and kind melody.
It makes you feel so safe and special and so much more relaxed to be here in this free open ocean.
Together you swim spiraling down and down into a marvelous and beautiful coral garden.

This coral reef garden has green seagrass with soft coral shining about with the most gorgeous colors.
You see so many types of fish.
Clownfishes, rainbowfishes and even angelfishes.
You swim down and down, and you see little tiny crabs of all different shapes, colors, and sizes.

You have now arrived at the legendary coral garden.
In the middle of the coral reef garden, resting in the center of these beautiful clams, is something that looks brown and shines with sparkles of metal.
It has seagrass growing on it and a peaceful seahorse resting on top of it.
As you get a little closer, you reach out and push the seagrass to the side.
Sitting in the middle of this circle of giant clams is what looks like to be the treasure chest.
It is wooden and has a brass gold lock keeping it shut firmly.
This must be Blackbeard's long-lost treasure chest.
You have found it!
Willy swims closer to you to help you.
He opens his enormous whale mouth, and he clutches the chest between his big whale teeth and begins to swim you both upwards.

You are holding onto his back so excitingly.
You two are now gliding and swimming back up to the surface going higher and higher together.
You are moving smoothly up towards the pirate ship that is just waiting calmly in the distance that is swaying and rocking over the waves.
Willy sends up a magnificent and victorious spurt of sea ocean spray from his blowhole.
The peaceful pirates have spotted you through their telescope.
Everyone is so happy to see you and is now cheering for your return.
With the little lock between Willy's teeth, he quickly breaks the lock and spits the chest out with a flip of his whale tail.
You are all able to open the chest now.

You and the peaceful pirates open the big heavy chest lid together.
You open it, and it looks like sunlight is glowing out from the inside.
It is the most dazzling light that is being reflected from the glorious treasure.
The treasure has so many magnificent and brilliant ancient artifacts, gold coins, mini statues, chalices,

precious gemstones, pearls, swords, and so many other treasures.

This is really a pirate's bounty.

You all have so much fun looking and feeling the treasure.

You all are leaping on the pirate ship and acting like real pirates.

You all are so happy, climbing up the mast and playing sword fighting.

You take the helm of the ship and have such amazing fun.

It feels so amazing and fantastic to be so free-spirited.

You are so happy to see all your new friends.

Willy stays for a while, laughing at all of you.

You all are being so silly with your treasure.

Willy also looks delighted too.

He gives you all a whale wave with his tail, gives a big spurt of seawater, and says goodbye.

You all wave and say thank you to the beautiful, gentle giant of the ocean.

With his huge mighty tail, he gives a big splash of water, and Willy disappears back beneath the waves of the ocean.

He continues to sing his lovely whale song.

Hmmm.
It is so soothing.
You start to feel so tired now.
So very tired as you climb back into the comfy hammock again.
You begin to rock along to the sounds of the ocean and the soothing whale songs of Willy the whale singing to you in the faraway distance.

As you rest here aboard the amazingly happy and loving pirate ship, you feel so much gratitude and love in your heart for Willy the whale.
He is such a kind hearted, generous and joyful creature to take you on your marvelous journey.
You two really have such an amazing time, and this is the greatest treasure of all.
As you begin to fall asleep now, you know that tomorrow you will wake up in your very own bed feeling so fresh and rested and so confident and happy inside.
So calm, confident, and happy to make your day tomorrow in the best possible way.

You are so courageous and brave.
You know that you can do anything in the world.
You are now drifting away, just sleeping and sleeping.
Floating and drifting into the most relaxing dreamland and just relax in that lovely land of pure magical dreams.

You are sleeping even deeper now.
Feeling so safe and so loved.
So blissfully wonderful to be the very special person that you are.
Sweat dreams.

42 minutes

CHAPTER 4

Wishing Waterfall

Now just lie down in your bed.
Make sure you get comfortable and listen along.
Just begin to relax more and more.
Let your sleepy and relaxing thoughts wonder about.
Now I would like for you to imagine visiting a very magical place.
An enchanted place where your every wish might soon come true.
If this sounds extra fun and extra relaxing to you, then you are in for a super special sleepy treat.
Very soon, all you need to do is to discover this very special magical wishing place.
Just close your eyes as you begin to use your wonderful imagination of yours just to relax more and more.

Let all of your daytime thoughts go as you begin to imagine and just dream.

It's becoming easier and easier to travel into your special dreamy place of wishes and really go there now.

Imagine a wonderful nighttime rainbow.

This rainbow takes you to a dream world full of possibilities that arrive as soon as you snuggle into sleep.

Just like a rainbow bridge that connects you to a far away distant land made up of many relaxing and beautiful colors.

The lovely rainbow pathway climbs all the way up into the sleepy nighttime sky above.

You can begin to imagine yourself on this wishing rainbow.

Now begin to imagine what your lovely rainbow bridge might look like.

You might even see your rainbow sparkle and glow with extra special wishing magic.

The fantastic rainbow bridge shines down on you.

It is so close beside you, shining down like a light beam all the way down through the stars of the night sky.

Maybe it shines down even through your own window.
It is almost as if you could reach out and feel these warm colors.
The light beams down on your hands and fingers.
You already know that this imaginary rainbow of yours is here to pick you up and float you along.
Very gently.
You are floating so happily.
Leading you all the way into the most enchanted and magical place at the end of this magical rainbow.

It is so soft and bouncy underneath your feet.
It is also very supportive.
It feels so safe and so strong.
Love imagining that you are walking, hopping, and bouncing on your rainbow.
You keep climbing up all the way into the sky.
Up and up you go until the rainbow bridge starts to bend back down again.
You are now moving down and down through the beautiful white fluffy clouds.
You are bending downwards on these light beams now.

You are going down and down even further until you see that there is a brand-new magical land full of magical wishes waiting here just for you.

You quickly realize that the rainbow has taken you all the way here.

All the way into the magical land of wishes that is suddenly below you.

You feel so excited now because your rainbow bridge has become like a curving slippery dip.

You sit down, and you slide, passing through the fluffy white clouds.

Suddenly you safely land, and you feel your feet touching the ground.

You feel yourself stepping down onto a soft green grassy hill landing so softly.

You find yourself stepping smoothly down and coming to a complete rest.

You are now sitting down happily underneath the shade of an enormous pink cherry blossom tree.

Now you look up and see this beautiful cherry blossom.

You must really be in the magical land of wishes.

Over behind the enormous cherry blossom, you can see a stunning enchanted waterfall flowing.

You know that this is the magical waterfall of wishes.
The waterfall of wishes has such clear and clean water.

It is almost as if it is a sparkling stream or a mist of shimmering magic in the air.

The water that falls here in the sparkling mist is the most gorgeous shade of blue that you have ever seen.

You now see even more magical colors streaming down as they all join with the clear blue water.

You now see shades of colors that you have never imagined before.

The magic of the waterfall glows brighter and brighter.

It shines even more marvelously the more you look at it.

You know that in your heart and in all of your thoughts, this impressive wishing magical waterfall has the power to bring your dream wishes to come right now to life.

Relax completely and rest.
Just be as calm and as happy as you wish to be, sitting peacefully under the pink cherry blossom tree.

You feel so happy and so relaxed.

It is as you haven't got a care in the world because the magical waterfall and your wishes are making it so.

Now you begin to wonder and imagine some of your most beautiful, most desired, and most favorite wishes coming true.

You gaze into this sparkly magical waterfall of wishes, and you decide to imagine just one of your happiest and kindest, most compassionate, most loving, and most exciting wishing coming true in real life now.

You know that this magical wishing waterfall only works for those wishes that are good, kind, loving, and the most helpful to everyone and especially if your wish makes you feel as happy as you can be.

The wishing waterfall will help you right now to this positive wish coming true.

Now, just imagine and start to make a wish.

Yes, just like that.

Go ahead and make your first special happy, loving wish.

As you do, what can you see?
What images or pictures does your happy wish look like?
Make it appear now in the magical mist of the wishing waterfall's beautiful colors.
Even as you wish it very quickly, you see the waterfall colors shine.
The magic mist of the waterfall sparkles.
You are seeing so many magical sparkles of the enchanting water bringing your happy, loving wish into real life now.
It is just like a movie.
You are watching more and more amazing details taking shape.
You see yourself joining with your wish.
You are now floating all the way into these happy, loving movie scenes.
You are now seeing yourself enjoying all the good scenes of your special wish.
You feel so good to also see yourself here in this magical happy movie.

You are now seeing yourself in all of these pictures and with all of these colors and even with all of the sounds and feelings, your special loving, happy wish.

It is brought into real life now.
You are seeing yourself feeling as happy as you wish yourself to be.
Now, as the waterfall glistens and shines, you keep feeling so very very happy.
Ask yourself if you have another special wish.
Imagine this wish coming true.
If you have another wish or even many have other wishes, you can wish for them now as long as these wishes are good and kind.
Just think of these wishes right now.

Very soon, you will see once again your magical wishing waterfall bringing every new wish clear into your life.
You see yourself joining into each happy scene feeling so good and being so very happy now as you just relax and continue to enjoy all of your special wishes coming true.
You are feeling so happy to continue exploring and to just keep making positive new wishes.
Imagine yourself moving into each of your amazing wishes.
Feel the loving and good wishes.
Always feeling better and better about yourself.

You are so much happier and positive to enjoy this incredibly special time in your life wishing your dreams.
Imagining yourself experiencing each wish coming into your life.

Now very soon, you are starting now to become so much sleepier.
You are feeling so very, very sleepy.
You know that it is time for you to sleep all the way into your bedtime dreams.
Take one last look at your waterfall of wishes feeling so happy to now be returning to your warm cozy bed.

You begin to see and feel the nighttime rainbow return.
All of the rainbow's light beams down to pick you up gently.
The rainbow bridge carries you all the way home.
All the way back down through your bedroom window.

You feel so happy and so calm all the way back into your warm and comfy bed.

As your body melts and relaxes, so do your thoughts. Relaxing soft into the soft mattress beneath you.

You feel your head resting on your pillow.

Your arms and legs feel so heavy now.

You are falling so happily and safely into your best sleep.

You are feeling so special and so loved as you drift deeper and deeper into your deep and happy dreams.

You will continue to dream with joyful delight.

You are dreaming about all of your most wonderful wishes coming true so very soon into your happiest life.

Sleep well now, and I wish you a sweet magical wishing waterfall dreams.

37 minutes

CHAPTER 5

Ancient Mountains

This sleep mediation is now going to take you on a fantastic and mysterious journey to meet a friendly dragon.
If you are ready to take the adventure to his hidden location high up the ancient mountains that are long forgotten, then close your eyes now.
Let your imagination run wild and free.
I want you to settle down into your bed.
I want you to get really comfortable.
Take a big deep breath in and a calm breath out.
You are doing amazing.
Take a deep breath in and a calm breath out.
Just breathe naturally and fully now.
You are feeling more and more relaxed.
You are doing great.

The meditation magic can only happy in the dreamy place of almost being awake and almost asleep.

Now imagine you are at a rocky mountain.
This mountain has a little bit of snow at the top.
These mountains are in a remote part of the world and are far away from where people live.
These are called the secret mountains that have not been explored yet by mankind for thousands of years.
Dragons are said that they no longer exist.
It is said that they have been driven to hide themselves at the most remote locations on Earth.
If you come by an abandoned cave far away from any human civilization, then it may just be the home of a dragon.

Imagine yourself walking along this mountain pass.
You have come here to search for the friendly dragon.
This narrow path along the mountains leads you up.
You know in your heart that you are very safe here.
It feels so fun to just explore the land.

The air feels so cool and refreshing, breezing across your face.
The landscape around you is so huge.
You can see the rocky mountains and rocky volleys as far as your eyes can see.
You have now made it pretty far up the mountain trail, and you start to see a massive castle built into the side of the mountain.
This castle looks abandoned, and vines are overgrowing on it.
Wow this place looks so fascinating and mysterious.
You notice a giant door where the entrance is located.
You feel so happy and excited.
Maybe this is where you will finally meet a friendly dragon.
You hope that this is where the friendly dragon lives.
You walk quietly up to the entrance of the cave and look inside.
A deep voice suddenly shouts out to you from within the castle.
It is like he already knew you were coming.
You shout back your name, and the deep voice calls out to you again.
Then suddenly, the cave starts to light up from deep within.
A golden light starts glowing all around you.

You can not see this dragon yet, but you step inside bravely and fearlessly.

You are so very confident and also curious.

You start walking through this massive cavern and twists and turns deeper and deeper into the mountainside.

There are wooden torches that start lighting up with fire all by themselves.

These start leading you through the darkness.

You still feel very safe here, and you know in your heart you will be protected.

As you follow and walk along, the cave opens up and gets bigger and bigger.

You immediately spot the dragon.

Such an immense, powerful creature with so many scales of so many colors.

He smiles and grins down on you.

Such a lovely big friendly grin.

He seems so very happy to finally see you.

You look at his scales, and they look so fascinating and interesting.

They all glimmer colorfully in the sparkling light.

His eyes are very shiny, and you can tell they are very kind.

As he moves towards you, you notice he has a tail.

He reaches out his claw to shake your hand.

You both laugh with happiness.

Wow you feel so lucky to meet a dragon in real life.
This is one of the rarest and most mythical creatures in the world.
Take a moment and just chat with the dragon.

You now look around his hidden cave.
He has jewels and gemstones all around the cave.
You see so many gold coins and giant piles of treasure.
This friendly dragon tells you it is wonderful to be blessed with such nice things.
Although these things do not make him truly happy.
Yes, it is wonderful to have all these wonderful things, but he prefers gemstones and crystals because they have such positive energy.
He gets a little lonely all by himself.
He tells you that he has always been feared throughout history and fought in battles, but he has learned to still love his life deep down in his heart.
He is so much wiser after learning this wisdom.
He now uses his fiery breath for only love and kindness.

The friendly wise dragon smiles down on you with such a friendly grin.
He asks if you want to go flying with him.
He wants to show you this land of his.
You are so excited and say oh yes please!
You climb up onto his back, and you hold onto his scales.
He has a lot of fluffy fur on the top of his back.
The dragon starts to walk along through the cave now.
He is taking big and heavy steps.
You two reach the opening of the cave, and sunlight starts to appear.
He now suddenly jumps into the air and takes you flying.
The dragon's wings are now spread wide and flaps effortlessly through the air.
He is laughing so hard and booming now with so much happiness and love.
You two soar through the sky.
You are holding on very tight to the dragon.
You feel so safe, so protected, and very powerful on your strong, friendly dragon friend.
The wind is rushing through your hair now, and you are feeling so free.
You are now flying over the land below you.

The dragon points out places and where he has been.
You feel so very lucky and free to be living in a great time of peace.
It is such a great time to be alive on the planet right now.
You are so very lucky.
For your first stop, you two are going to explore the abandoned castle again near the mountain.
The dragon flies over the drawbridge onto the castle floor.
Wow, it is so fun to have this castle all to yourself.
You two walk inside and find a banquet room in the castle.
You find so many stairways and passages leading you out of the mountain top.
Wow this is so amazing.
You now hop back onto the back of your dragon friend.
Now you two explore the far reaches of Earth.
You two fly over tropical islands, see volcanoes, and even all the way up to the snowy tops of mountains.
You may now keep flying with your dragon flying over the planet.
You two explore everywhere with your new dragon friend.

Have as much fun in the world visiting some of the most amazing places.
When my voice returns, it will be time for you to have the most peaceful and happiest dreams.

After you have had the most wonderful and magical time with your dragon friend, it is now time for you to return home.
It is now nighttime, and the moon is shining high in the nighttime sky.
The dragon flies through the air.
He has such strong wings.
He is taking you all the way home.
You give him such a big hug.
You slide down his arm and into your bedroom window.
You wave goodbye to your dragon friend.
He gives you his big happy smile and then flaps his wings and flies off into the nighttime sky.
You now smile to yourself as you watch your dragon friend fly off into the night.
He is flying back to his cave in the mountains, to his home.
You now climb into bed and snuggle down under the warm blankets.

You breathe in a big deep sigh of gratitude and happiness.
This was such an amazing adventure.
Sleepiness is now taking over.
You are going to be lulled off into the most beautiful dreams.
You are going to dream and sleep so deeply now.
You feel so happy, so free, and safe.
You know that you are very powerful and confident.
You know that you can do anything.
You such an amazing and positive energy in your heart.
You are so wise, kind, and just like your dragon friend, you drift off into the most wonderful dreams.
You feel so blessed and loved.
You know that you can visit your dragon friend at anytime you want in his mountain side cave.
You can visit anytime you wish.
Sweet dragon dreams.

31 minutes

CHAPTER 6

African Safari Adventure

Welcome to the lion adventure journey for this part of the book.

This is a sleep meditation where you will be taken on a magical and mystical guided meditation adventure across the African savannah.

On this journey, you will meet extraordinary animals who will show the circle of life and for all that lives within.

If you are ready to have the most amazing journey with some fun, fascinating, and loving animals, then close your eyes and let your imagination run free.

Imagine you are now in a great big green African savannah plain.

This is where the animal kingdom roams free.

This is sacred land and is the home of the lions.

These lions only rule the land with strength and wisdom.
Imagine you are standing here in the African savannah.
You look around you, but you can't seem to spot any animals yet.
Just plain open grasslands.
Wow is it so relaxing.
Now take some deep breaths in and out fully.
In and out fully.
That's amazing.
You are doing wonderful.

You now easily imagine a fresh and gentle breeze of wind blowing across your face and into your hair.
The ground is soft and warm underneath your feet.
There is a lot of space all around you.
You see vast stretches of open land, making you feel so free.
You are filled with strength and courage.
You have so much curiosity, and you discover and suddenly see a huge tree in the distance.
You start walking towards it, and you feel something very warm next to you and brushes up onto you.
It is a lion!

This lion is not a fully grown lion yet but still bigger than a cub.
He has a little soft mane and such a friendly smile.
He looks so kind and silly, and you laugh along with him.
You both laugh, and he tells you he is headed in the same direction to the Tree of Life.
Wow, you feel so lucky to have such a great companion with you, and you feel so happy.
Walk and talk to your new friend.
He tells you his name, and you feel so happy and relaxed.
You two travel onward together towards the Tree of Life.
It is standing all by itself.
As you and your lion friend get closer, you now see that this is a very ancient and magical tree.
It has an extra thick tree trunk despite being on the warm and dry savannah grassland.
This tree has healthy, luscious, and green leaves.
It has such a great and wonderful energy about it.

There is a round patch ring of fresh green grass growing around the base of the tree.
You are admiring the grass and the tree as you walk around it.

You notice something quite extraordinary.
On the other side of the tree, sitting on the grass, is a baboon meditating.
You can't help but look and observe this baboon.
He has a red nose and blue cheeks.
He has a little patch of white hair on his head and looks old and very wise.
He is sitting cross-legged and is deep within his thoughts, just meditating.
He suddenly opens his eyes wide open, leaps up to you, and shakes your hand so vigorously.
He also pats your lion friend and welcomes you both with so much love, joy, and kindness.
He climbs up the tree, goes inside the hollow tree, and gestures you both to follow him inside.
You listen and follow him with excitement.
This is the baboon shaman, a mystical healer with so much wisdom, knowledge, and positive energy.
He knows the sacred knowledge about the planet.
You see, he has drawings of animals, lions, weather patterns, and ancient paintings explaining the circle of life all over his walls.
The paintings are explaining that this life energy flows and connects all living things and all living creatures.
Everything lives together in perfect respectful harmony generation after generation.

You immediately understand the balance of the ecosystem, and every single living thing and animal has a right to live peacefully in each of their habitats. The baboon breaks open an orange fruit to share with the both of you.

You can ask the baboon anything you wish to know. You can ask him anything you want.

Spend a couple of moments and chat with the old and wise baboon.

You feel so special and so honored to have visited this ancient tree and the shaman baboon.

He explains to you and your lion friend that he will make a great kind-hearted king one day.

You both wave goodbye to the wise baboon, and you both travel onwards to the jungle in the distance.

You now see a shallow river that flows along and trickles and winds through the African savannah and to the jungle ahead of you.

The water is so soothing and so crystal clear.

You both now enter under the shade of the cool jungle trees.

This tropical jungle has so many exotic plants and flowers.

You feel so very peaceful here and so welcomed.

The stream then turns into a tiny waterfall that crashes down into a blue pond.

Wow how beautifully refreshing this is.

You now see the most interesting animal just standing on a rock above the tiny pond.

You see its paws and chin are raised and moving his little head about.

It is a meerkat!

Wow, he is so funny and so cute.

You now start to hear branches breaking and footsteps stomping.

Suddenly a little warthog just jumps out and emerges from the jungle trees.

Then he jumps up, belly flops into the blue crystal clear pond, splashes water everywhere, and soaks the meerkat in water.

They both laugh, and you two go up to them to talk to them.

You and the lion become friends with the meerkat and warthog.

They are so funny, silly, and so jolly good to be around.

You all have so much fun together despite being such an odd group of individuals.

You all have fun adventures in the jungle, and they teach you everything they know.

Just relax, have fun, and just think positive.

You all then meet a female lioness who is so lovely and is friends with your lion friend.

Just have a few moments and just have fun with everyone here.

It is now nighttime, and your lion friend senses that it is now time to return home.

You all travel together back to the lion's home and across all of the lands in the savannah.

You all walk into the beautiful African sunset with your new friends.

Two lions, one warthog, a meerkat, and a very happy human all loving each other's company.

You now know that we can all live so happily and peacefully together in such harmony.

You now look ahead of you to the sunset.

You see in the distance, the wise old baboon is waiting for all of you.

You all have made it home.

Your lion friend has now fulfilled his destiny to become king.

This is the most sacred ceremony in the animal kingdom.

This ceremony uplifts your spirits and inspires you to do anything you want because you have a very special place in this circle of life.

Kindness, friendliness, wisdom, and love are all of the supreme sacred powers of positive energy that always prevails no matter what.

There is now a great massive celebration as all of the lions in the pride rejoice, having the new rightful king now returning home.

All of the animals in the kingdom arrive and circle around you all, and dance to the music.

All of the animals are celebrating together in such an amazing, fun, and peaceful way.

All delighted and feeling so blessed to have had such a fantastic meditation adventure with these beautiful animals.

It is now time for you to return to your warm and cozy bed.

This is where you will now dream deeply and sleep very peacefully now.

You will be in such bliss in your mind and heart.

You know that you are now a part of a very special place in the circle of life.

You belong with everything, and you are so very very loved.

You are now drifting off to have the happiest and most wonderful dreams.

You smile to yourself and know that you can visit your African savannah friends anytime you want for another amazing meditation adventure.

Sweet dreams.

20 minutes

CHAPTER 7

Magic Crystal Island

Now imagine a place where anything is possible.
This is a place where the most amazing things can happen to you right before your eyes.
This is the guided meditation for you to explore on your very own private and magical tropical island.
Close your eyes now and relax your entire body.
Remember that the meditation magic can only happen in that dreamy place of being almost awake and almost asleep.
Now imagine yourself standing on the shore of a beautiful tropical island.
You easily imagine the warm sand warming up your toes.
You look at the blue ocean in front of you.
The ocean is sparkling and glittering in the sunlight.

You watch the gentle and beautiful waves flow onto the sand and then out back into the ocean.
Take a deep breath in and a calm breath out.
Breath just like the flow of the waves of the ocean.
Each breath flowing in and out.
Just like the waves of the ocean.
Wow that is so wonderful.
You are doing amazing.

You now find yourself standing on your very own magical private tropical island.
It is so relaxing and peaceful here.
You feel so excited.
You know in your heart that there is so much for you to discover and explore here.
You start walking across the soft, warm sand beneath your feet.
A magical and gorgeous bird flies down to greet you.
It waves its wings to you and has the most colorful and pretty feathers you have ever seen.
What colors do you see on this bird's feathers?
The bird chirps proudly that he is the bird of paradise.
He will guide you around the island and show you everything there is to know.

This is your animal guide on this tropical island.
What is his name?
It can be any name that you wish to call him.
Your bird guide tells you that this tropical island is your special and safe place from now on.
You feel so very peaceful, and your heart is so full of joy.
You start walking through the palm trees, and you can see the magnificent sight before your eyes.
There is a beautiful and stunning waterfall.
The water splashes into a strong and gentle river glittering and shimmering in the sunlight.
The water looks so enchanting, and you watch as this waterfall is flowing so easily.
You feel so calm, and you suddenly notice that there are shiny rocks just hovering in the air.
It is flowing down little waterfalls.
Wow this is so amazing.
This is definitely an enchanting place to be in.
You can feel the healing energy of this place so easily here.
Everything is happening in perfect harmony now.
This your private tropical island of only pure peace, love, happiness, and magic.
As you look around the waterfall, you notice there are what looks like magical plants growing here.
The plants are so huge, tropical, and exotic.

They have such bright and amazing colors.
Wow it is so beautiful and marvelous.
Your bird guide tells you that there are also many animals living on your island.
Some of the animals you may have seen before, and some of them are magical creatures.
What animals do you want to see here on your tropical island?

Now your bird guide takes and leads you to the wishing cavern.
It is a very sacred and magical cave.
This is where anything is possible.
You walk through the wishing cavern and feel so very very special.
It is radiating and glittering with so much life energy.
It is glowing pink with sparkling rose quartz crystals.
There are so many crystals here radiating positive energy.
You are now standing in the middle of the cave and make a wish that is close to your heart.
You say your wish out loud now.
Your wish echoes through and around the cave.
All of the crystals start to light up with magical and positive energy.

Wow this is amazing.

Suddenly all of the crystals start growing bigger and bigger, rising up into the air.

Then a big piece of crystal flies over you like a hoverboard.

It seems like it wants you to step on it to go flying.

You step onto your magic crystal board, and you start flying out of the cave.

Your bird guide is flying along next to you, gliding through the air.

The wind is rushing through your face and hair now.

You are now flying over your tropical island.

You are soaring, dipping, and floating through the air, going faster and faster.

You look down at your beautiful island with such a stunning landscape.

Your bird guide is still flying right by your side.

You both laugh together with so much joy and happiness.

Wow this is so much fun.

You feel so light as a feather.

You feel so free.

You are flying on your magical crystal board.

You are exploring your very own magical tropical island.

Have some time to just fly and soar through the air.

Take some time to fly and float about.

Keep exploring and discover everything about this magical island.
When my voice returns, it will be time for you to have some deep and relaxing dreams.

You are feeling very sleepy now.
You have decided it is now time for you to return back home to your warm and cozy bed.
You and your magical crystal fly down through the air.
You hop off of your magical crystal board and onto the warm sand on the tropical island.
You now wave and say goodbye to your friendly bird guide.
The island now suddenly just starts to fade around you.
It is becoming cloudier and cloudier.
You can only see clouds of white around you.
Then the mist suddenly clears, and you find yourself back in your comfortable and safe room.
You are falling fast asleep now.
You feel so grateful for this incredible journey on your very own magical tropical island.

You now can start to just drift into your coziest and happiest dreams.

You are now falling fast asleep, going deeper and deeper.

You feel so special, so powerful, and so very loved.

You know that in your heart that this is your magical island.

It will always be here waiting just for you anytime you wish.

Sweet magical island dreams.

25 minutes

CHAPTER 8

Koala Grove

Hello and welcome to another relaxing and sleepy meditation.
This is an enchanting bedtime story that will take you on a fantastic journey.
Listen to my voice at it will guide you to the biggest island in the world.
Which is Australia.
Australia is home to some of the most amazing, exotic, cuddliest, fluffiest, and sleepiest animals on Earth.
Are you ready to meet all of the cutest animals in the world?
Amazing! I am too!
Now I want you just settle in and get very comfortable and cozy.

Close your eyes now and let your imagination run wild and free.
Think to yourself about how much you love animals.
Take a deep breath in and a long calm breath out.
Now just let your breathing continue to do this naturally all by itself.
Feel your body just relaxing.
Awesome, you are doing fantastic.

Now imagine you are in the Australian rainforest.
Imagine looking around and seeing big green trees and sunny blue skies.
Take in and breathe the beautiful fresh, crisp air.
You instantly feel at peace here.
You may have heard there is an old legend in Australia about a secret safe haven that is hidden deep within the land.
This haven is where the most cutest, cuddliest, and amazing koalas live.
This mystical place is called the Koala Grove.
This is a place where vast amounts of eucalyptus trees grow to protect the koalas from the outside world, even from forest rangers and nature lovers.
It is even hidden from bird watchers who have binoculars.

None of these people have been able to find this place because the exotic birds and clever kangaroos distract them on purpose to lead them off of the path.

The aborigine people were the first native people of Australia.

These people have lived here for thousands and thousands of years.

They know and understand the land's sacred energy, and they respect the circle of life here.

This safe Koala haven is so mystical and mysterious, and the Aborigines are the only ones who know the secret location.

The most skilled and expert Aboriginal trackers know that way to the haven.

You now breathe deeply in and use all of your senses now to help you discover your way to Koala Grove that is located in the heart of the Australian land.

You now spot a little honey-eating bird.

This bird is so tiny and just buzzes around with so much energy.

It has a yellow chest and hovers in front of you.

To your surprise, it can fly backward!

Only a few birds in the whole world can do this.

This bird zigzags back and forth.
Its tiny wings are just humming with so much vibrant energy.
You realize that this bird is trying to show you the way and to follow it.
You follow it for a while, and the honeyeater drinks nectar from the sweet flowers around you.

As you start to explore the land even more, you notice some very delicate purple wildflowers growing in a line.
It looks like it is a secret trail between the trees that are revealing the way to you.
You follow the purple flowers.
Then through the trees, you come to a water hole.
It looks so refreshing and relaxing.
You look at the crystal blue aqua water just gleaming in the sunlight like a turquoise gem.
Wow it is so beautiful.
This pond is covered with vibrant green lily pads with beautiful blooming flowers of white and pink all over it.

You look over the pond to see what's behind it.
It looks like it is shrouded in a white, soft mist making everything so hazy and cloudy.
It is tough to see, but you smell the eucalyptus trees stronger than ever before.
You realize that this could be a clue.
Koalas love to eat the leaves of eucalyptus trees.
You trust your senses, and you follow the wildflowers trail and the scent of eucalyptus trees and go into the mist.

You now arrive at the Koala haven.
It is a dense grove of the strongest, freshest and healthiest trees with the most amazing leaves and so many happy koalas.
These are probably the happiest koalas in the world.
An older grandpa koala crawls and waddles over to you.
He welcomes you to the Koala grove so kindly.
You look around you in awe and amazement.
You look at all of the adorable koalas around you, just relaxing with their families and just eating on the trees munching on the leaves, and just relaxing in the sunshine.

The grandpa koala tells you that these koalas love to sleep, but no other koala likes to more than me.
I sleep all day, and I am only awake for two hours to just eat some leaves and hang out with my family and friends here in the Koala Grove.
Here is the sleepiest and cuddliest tree.
You poke your head around the tree, and you see so many koalas just sleeping their day away.
They look so safe, so protected just being in their favorite spots.
This makes you feel so happy, and you just admire how cute and adorable all of these koalas are.
They all look so fluffy.
It makes your heart swell up with so much joy.
They all look like little cuddly fluffy teddy bears.
You just want to hold them all.

You notice that one of the koalas starts to blink his eyes and opens them.
He looks at you with such dreamy eyes making you feel so very sleepy.
You just want to doze off with them.
The koala smiles at you with his little mouth under his cute nose.

He waves his little paw at you, and you feed him leaves.

He starts to munch on them so lazily.

You gently reach out your hand and pat his soft fluffy furry head and feel his fluffy ears.

The koala reaches out to you and climbs onto your chest, wrapping around you with the coziest and warmest hug you have ever had.

You feel so blissfully happy and so peaceful.

You are hugging the cutest koala as he just nestles down sleepily on you like a big warm, soft teddy bear.

You feel so relaxed and starting to feel a little sleepy now.

With the koala dozing off, you are starting to feel dreamy as well.

You pet his soft, gentle fur and place him back to the spot on the tree where he was before.

You lie down on the grass below, and you take a nap.

You start to drift off into one of your happiest and most wonderful sleep safely in the comfort of the Koala Grove.

You are with your kind, sleepy, and loving koala friends.

You are feeling so very peaceful and proud that you trusted your instincts to lead you to this perfect place.

This place is so warm, calm, and cozy.

When my voice returns, you will have dozed off safely in the most blissful sleep like a koala.

I hope you have happy dreams, and may it be blissful and beautiful.

19 minutes

CHAPTER 9

Wolf Guardian

Welcome to this guided meditation to help you fall asleep.

This adventure is where your snow wolf will take you on a magical and mystical journey through the snowy mountains across the ice lands and winter forests.

If you are ready to meet your amazing and loyal guardian wolf, then close your eyes now and make sure you are ready to just relax and let your imagination run wild and free.

Now imagine yourself in a huge white snowfield that is surrounded by many trees.

Now imagine as you look around, you see there is no one else but you here just enjoying nature.

The air feels fresh, crisp, and cool.

You take a deep breath in and a long calm breath out.

One more time, take a deep breath in and a long calm breath out.

Feel your body relax as your breathing goes back to its natural rhythm.

That is amazing.

You are doing fantastic.

Perfect.

You are enjoying the open snowy nature space here in this big snowfield.

It is very peaceful here.

You now can easily imagine that it is around afternoon time and the sun is starting to set behind the snowy forest trees in the distance.

The sky is turning to twilight.

You walk through the snowy field, and you realize you have a long wool gray coat around your shoulders and snow boots on your feet to keep your feet and toes very warm.

Now you notice there are a small logs crackling and burning.

Perhaps this fire was started by people.

You still continue on in your journey but think hmm how mysterious.

The fire's embers are starting to die out as all of the wooden logs burn down in small orange flames.

You watch the smoke rise from the fire and twirls and curls in the air into the open snowy air.

Now you see through the smoke, and you see an outline of an animal.

This animal has bright eyes and watches you carefully and intently.

The beast steps forwards, and you see that it is your majestic and beautiful wolf guardian.

He looks so strong and healthy.

He has thick white fur to make sure he can withstand the cold and has a very kind and happy face.

This snow wolf is really big.

Wow he is so calm and brave.

You know that deep down, he is very wise and loyal.

This is a very special creature of mother nature.

You feel so lucky to be meeting your very own guardian wolf.

You reach out to touch his fur and say hello.

It circles around you and the fire without ever taking its eyes off of you.

Then it comes over next to you and bows its head.

You have so much happiness in your heart.
You pet this divine creature, and it has such soft white fur.
It now crouches down, and you sense that it wants you to climb onto its back.
You immediately climb on its back, and you can feel that he has magnificent strength.
You feel so very safe and so protected with your amazing new wolf friend.

You hold onto the wolf's lovely fluffy fur, and this wonderful creature takes you walking through the white snow.
It now starts to run gently, and you feel so much joy as your wolf breaks into a sprint.
It is streaking across the snow, running faster than you could ever think possible.
The cool crisp air rushes over your face and through your hair.
You feel so alive and so excited.
Your loyal wolf friend takes you to explore the icy wilderness.

Together you both run wild and free as you hold on tightly to the wolf's back.
It runs all across the snowfields and through the icy forest.
You notice that it has great instincts and intuition, and he fully trusts them and himself.
He navigates this icy wilderness with so much ease and wisdom.
You notice snow owls perched up in the trees, and they are all staring down at you with kind eyes.
Your wolf gives them a friendly nod as you both run by them.
You are now running past a completely frozen lake.
You notice and pass some huge polar bears looking for fish to eat.
They notice you, and they look so happy as they wave their paws to you.
Your wolf runs so quickly.
He is such a brave wolf.

After riding across the ice landscapes for quite some time, you stop by a mountain river with water trickling and rushing down made from the melted snow caps.
You cup your hands, and you drink the pure cold mountain water.

Wow it tastes so amazing, so fresh, and so clean.
It quenches your thirst and uplifts your mood and spirits.
Now your wolf friend starts drinking from the stream as well.
You feel so happy and lucky to have such a loyal companion with you.
You feel so spiritually connected to this amazing creature.
You know that this is an animal in your heart that you can tell all of your secrets to and truly trust with your biggest dreams, wishes, and deepest desires.

Your wolf guardian crouches down to you and nods for you to go on his back again for a final ride.
You are so curious and excited about where he is going to take you next.
You hold on tightly and give a pat on the wolf's back.
He now suddenly sprints up the mountainside and climbs up the mountain.
At the very top of this icy mountain, you see the most amazing and stunning view across the snowy countryside.
Wow it is absolutely breathtaking.
You see all the forests, lakes, waterfalls, and ice caps below.

At the top of this mountain, there is a gigantic tree.
It is the biggest tree you have ever seen.
You hop off your wolf guardian, and you walk up to look and admire the tree.
Suddenly you see wolf cubs playing about, just tumbling and chasing each other around in the snow.
You then notice there are also many other wolves just relaxing, resting, and gathered around this massive tree.
Your guardian wolf friend has taken you to meet his wolfpack.
They live at the very top of the mountain at the base of the giant tree.
You understand the wolf is showing how important loyalty and trust is, by bringing you to his home.
Now you suddenly feel such a deep bond with him, and you now know that you are always safe here whenever you need inspiration.
Trust your instincts, be brave, make wise choices, and remember you are always free and safe.
Some wolf cubs now run over to you, and you pet and play with them.
They are so cute and fluffy.
They make you laugh so much.

The moon has come out now, and it is a full moon.
The wolves all start to howl together in the moonlight.
You join them in a howl.
You feel so powerful and alive to really express your true self.
Your spirit soars with so much freedom and fun.
You feel so much gratitude and happiness for this amazing adventure.
You now know that it is time for you to return home.
You give your guardian wolf one last pet behind the ears and wave goodbye to everyone on the icy landscape.
Everything starts to fade around you, and you return to your warm and cozy bed.

You know in your heart that your loyal wolf guardian will always be there for you to visit anytime you wish.
Just smile and be happy to yourself, knowing this while you drift into your most wonderful and blissful dreams.
Sleep deeply now and feel so relax and wonderful.
You feel so brave, powerful, wise, kind, loved, and so inspired.

Now I wish you all of the happiest and sweetest dreams tonight.

17 minutes.

CHAPTER 10

Puppy Kingdom

Make yourself comfortable and close your eyes.
Take a big deep breath in through your nose.
And slowly and gently breathe out through your mouth.
Again big deep breath in and slowly and gently breathe out through your mouth.
One more time, big deep breath in and slowly and gently breathe out through your mouth.

Just relax and let your breathing come back to its natural rhythm.
Now I want you to imagine you are in a beautiful luscious green meadow field.

Flowers are growing all around the edges of this meadow field.

You can tell parts of this field have very young grass growing.

You can see the grass and plants blowing in the gentle breeze.

Here you are safe, loved, and well-protected always.

Take a look around you.

What else can you see?

Take a good look around.

You can hear rustling up ahead of you in the long green grass.

You wonder what it could be.

The grass is still moving about, so you set out to take a look.

You walk towards the moving grass, and what do you see?

You found a little black cute puppy.

It is all by itself on this big green field!

Well, it seems to be having such a great time just rolling about in the grass.

You watch the puppy just for a moment while it is having so much fun.

You watch it as it chases its own tail.

It is trying so hard to catch it.

You see a spot of white fur on one of its paws.

You decide to name the dog spot.

It suddenly stops because it sees you standing there just looking at it.
You don't want to frighten it anymore, so very gently, you reach out your hand for the little puppy to have a sniff so it won't be afraid of you.
The puppy seems to really like you!
It starts to jump up and down with so much excitement and starts licking you all over.
You gently pet and stroke the puppy's fur.
It feels so soft underneath your hand.
You now sit down and play with the little puppy.

You and the cute little puppy start to roll around in the grass, having such a fantastic time.
You are kind of worried that why is this little puppy all by itself.
Well maybe it is lost, but you hope it is not.
Then another dog just like him pops out of the long grass.
This dog looks just like the puppy but a lot bigger.
You realize that this dog is the puppy's mother.
She has been looking for her baby all over the place.
She runs up to the puppy and snuggles him so much.
Now the little puppy is so happy.

The puppy starts jumping all over its mother, and the mother looks at you with such loving and kind eyes.
Then all of a sudden, she talks to you.
You are absolutely shocked and flabbergasted.
This beautiful dog just spoke!
Oh my god!
You notice the mother has the same white spot as the little puppy.
They look so cute together.
She tells you that her name is Sweety.
Her puppy's name is Sam.
The little puppy is a boy, and she is so thankful to you for looking after her puppy.
She invites you to join them to a special place where other humans do not know about.
It is called the puppy kingdom.
She tells you to follow her, and you happily do.

You walk through the long and tall green grass.
You feel the bushes against your legs.
The little puppy sam is so happy and just rushes ahead of you.
He looks like he is having the time of his life, just smiling.

After a short while, you all come to a little white picket fence with a gate in the middle of it.
Sweety opens the gate, and you see on the other side is an absolutely amazing view.
It looks like a very large castle with so many details.
The whole castle is painted black with white spots all over it.

There is a pathway that leads to the castle.
You all follow it, and it takes you to the most amazingly large castle doors that you have ever seen.
They are gigantic and enormous.
The doors are also black with white spots on them.
It kind of looks like Sam and Sweety.
The big doors open up for you as if it was open by magic.
You step through to the other side, and you see what looks like a gigantic house of fun and play.
You can see so many bright and wonderful colors everywhere.
Wow it is so majestic and wonderful here.

In this castle, there are so many different sizes and breeds of dogs.
Big ones, small ones, thin ones, chubby ones.
There are so many dogs!
Pugs, beagles, golden retrievers, rottweilers, poodles, German shepherds, and so many more.
Sweety tells you that this is a castle that is solely run by dogs and puppies.
They even have their own king.
He has a very deep, commanding voice and is married to the queen.
This is a palace of pure fun and enjoyment.
Here is where you will be treated like royalty.
Oh how lovely.
Sweety tells you that you can take a good look around if you want to.
There are food, snacks, and drinks you can enjoy.
Wow you are feeling so lucky.
You now spot some small dogs all having fun and sliding down what looks like a big waterslide.
They all look like they are having so much fun.
You see a big swimming pool with some more dogs just swimming and playing about.
You see other dogs jumping off the diving boards and disappearing beneath the water.
Everyone looks like they are having so much fun.
You decide to enter the palace now yourself.

You really want to see what else is inside here.

Wow there are so many great things here.
The first thing that catches your eye is the racetrack.
It runs right through the palace and loops around back in the gardens.
There is a game room with everything you could possibly imagine here.
There is a trampoline, and you see dogs just flying so high above you doing some fantastic acrobatic tricks.
Wow it kind of looks scary and dangerous.
There is so much to do here.
Your head is spinning with so many options.
It is now your turn to go around the palace and do whatever you want.
Maybe you can play ball, swim in the pool, have fun on the waterslide, or jump on the trampoline.
Whatever you want to do, you can do it here.
Don't forget to eat the food and snacks.
So just for a little bit, decide where you want to go and what you would like to explore.
It is now time for you to have lots and lots of fun.

Did you have fun playing with all of your new puppy friends?

Did you see and experience all of the things you would like to?

Did you get yourself a snack and food?

You are feeling a bit sleepy now.

You wonder if you could just get some rest, and you notice Sam is sleepy as well.

He is even having a hard time keeping his eyes open.

Even Sweety is looking very tired as well.

Now all of you walk into another very large room.

This room is the biggest dog bed there has ever been.

It is the size of a small house.

Oh my it is so massive!

It is made up of the softest fur and has the biggest and softest cushions made up of feathers, and you know it was made just for you to lie down on.

Sweety gestures to the two of you that it is time for a little nap.

You both jump into a big soft dog bed and get really comfortable.

There are so many dogs here too.

You now just close your eyes and take a big deep breath in, and you slowly and gently breathe out.

You are so happy and so loved to be with Sam and his mom.

You are so happy you have met all of the other lovely puppies.
Your eyes are feeling very heavy now.
You really don't want to open them now, but that is totally okay.
You don't feel like you want to anyways.
Just lie here for a little while now.
A little snooze and nap never hurt anyone.
Just lie here and be safe.
You now know that you can always come back here to the puppy kingdom to see your new friends whenever you wish.
Just snuggle up next to Sam, and when you finally wake up, you will be in your very own bed.
You are feeling so refreshed, happy, and ready to start the new day when you wake up.

30 minutes

CHAPTER 11

Owl Spirit

Welcome to this special guided meditation where you will meet with your wise spirit animal.
Close your eyes now and take a big deep breath in and a long calm breath out.
That's amazing.
Feel your breath moving in and out like the waves of the ocean.
It is so simple and relaxing.
Just breath.
Feel your whole body starting to relax now as you prepare to meet your wise and powerful spirit animal.
Imagine a big green forest with giant ancient and wise trees.

This forest is shrouded in mist and knows everything about the history of the Earth.
Nature always remembers everything because energy is passed from one generation to the next.
These ancient and wise trees are home to an extraordinary and intelligent creature.
This creature is blessed with the wisdom to see everything and understand everything from the highest perspective.
It knows and will teach you how to be kind to yourself and kind to others.
It believes in the divine balance of the universe.
Imagine you are standing here in this misty forest.
You feel the soft green grass beneath your feet.
You can smell the damp Earth.
You can see the leaves and flowers of this ancient forest, and you feel a cool crisp, refreshing breeze blowing against your face.

You now spot a particular tree that has branches on the ground, twisting and turning.
The branches look like it is leading you up to the thick green leaves above.
You get a feeling that you should climb this tree.
Follow this inner voice in your heart, this feeling in your belly.

This is your intuition talking to you.
Listen to it.
You start to climb the tree with ease.
You feel so happy and so free-spirited.
You love climbing this tree and feeling the smooth and rough bark against your hands.
You find footholds to climb up and branches to cling on to.
You start to climb higher and higher.
You feel so special and so excited.
You are at one with this tree.
You are truly apart of nature now, and you feel like you belong here in the branches of this ancient tree.

Suddenly you have a strong feeling that you are being watched.
You look around you and see huge orange eyes looking at you from behind the leaves.
These eyes are so captivating and seems like it is hypnotizing you.
You could stare into these eyes all day.
You feel so curious and reach to push the leaves aside.
You see that these big orange eyes are from an owl.
You realize that this is a magical owl and one of the largest owls on the planet.

It looks so incredible and amazing.
It has such feathery wings and a lovely white coat.
It still looks at you with its golden orange eyes.
You know that the owl has excellent eyesight.
You sense that this owl can see beyond just sight.
He has the ability to see and feel everything with his mind.
It can sense instincts and intuitions.
You feel so connected to this owl.
This owl makes you feel like it is your best friend or even a family member.
You are so calm, so peaceful, so safe, and so loved here in the branches with your new owl friend.

You realize that this owl is your spirit animal.
It will guide you and protect you.
It will also help you discover your own wisdom and power.
Does your spirit animal have a name?
The wisdom of the owl connects with you.
You may ask it anything you want.
You may ask it for some advice.
Or you may even want to ask whatever it is you wish to know.
Feel your thoughts and answers clarify in your mind.

After talking to your spirit animal for a bit with your mind, it asks if you would want to go for a fly over the forest.

Wow how exciting this would be!

You are so honored and say yes with so much joy in your heart.

The owl blinks his eyes three times, and suddenly golden enchanted sparkles light up around the owl.

It is now growing bigger and bigger and now big enough for you to climb onto its back!

Hold on tightly to some of his fluffy feathers.

Wow he feels so soft and smooth.

You now both go up, flying higher and higher up and away.

You both are flying so freely now high up over the ancient treetops.

You feel so free and powerful.

It feels like you can do anything.

From here in the sky, you can see the sun setting on the horizon.

Wow such a magical view with just a little bit of warm orange daylight left.

Is there a special place you would like your spirit guide to take you?

Wherever you wish to go or whatever you wish to see.

Think about it in your heart now, and your owl will fly you there.

Is there anything else you would to ask your owl?
As you fly together soaring through the sky, you are able to ask it anything you wish.
You both fly over a lake that is glowing blue between the trees.
Together you both glide and soar over a waterfall, and it is flowing so peacefully down and into a little river.
You both now fly over the mystical and ancient mountains.
Wow these are so beautiful and magnificent, with everything covered in dark green.

It is now nighttime now, and you notice the moon is high up in the sky.
The stars have come out to shine and play, sparkling and lighting up the darkness around you.
The starlight is twinkling down over the ancient forest.
The owl now flies you home.
Together, you are still soaring through the sky and back to your room, where you are now relaxing so peacefully and happy.
You pet the soft feather and beautiful coat of this extraordinary animal spirit guide before it flies off.

You say a big thank you in your mind because you know that your spirit animal is always watching out for you.

It will always be there to guide you with all the wisdom, kindness, love, and strength.

Your spirit animal is always ready to share its universal wisdom with you.

You feel so relaxed and sleepy now.

You feel so safe, so peaceful, and filled with so much happiness in your heart.

Sweet dreams.

20 minutes

CHAPTER 12

Limiting Belief Buster

Many of the limiting beliefs we have stem from our childhood.
Children are young and can be shaped and molded by their surroundings with relative ease.
If we can successfully program our subconscious mind with ideas of success, confidence, and self love, then there is no limit to what we can achieve in life.
Here in this last part of the audiobook is a list of affirmations that should be played on repeat and even can be recited as repetitions is sure way to program our subconscious mind.
Play this for you and your child all night on a low comfortable volume, and you can even repeat it throughout the entire day.

Use these affirmations for 31 days or longer for the best results.
I am wise, brilliant and wonderful.
I love myself deeply.
I believe in my ability to succeed.
I am smart.
I am brilliant.
I am intelligent.
I am a fast learner.
Learning is fun and exciting.
I read, write and learn very quickly.
I have many gifts and talents.
I make wise decisions.
I enjoy eating healthy foods.
I am destined to live a life of prosperity.
My thoughts create my world.
All is well in my world.
I think positive thus creating a positive world.
My positive attitude attracts positive situations and positive circumstances.
What I think about often eventually becomes my reality.
I attract situations that matches how I feel.
I visualize what I want often.
I talk about what I want often.
I think about what I want often.
I am a kind and generous person.

I show compassion towards others.
I treat people how I want to be treated.
What I do to others I actually do to myself.
I take my schoolwork very seriously.
I am dedicated to being a wonderful student.
There isn't anything that I cannot be, do or have.
I excel in my academics.
I am a natural born leader.
I am strong fit and athletic.
My mind is powerful and I use it wisely.
I am safe.
I am loved.
I am friendly.
I am brave.
I am courageous.
I am a winner.
I am very creative.
I believe in myself.
I trust my abilities.
I am confident.
I make friends easily.
I am a good person.
I am a good friend.
I always overcome my challenges.
I believe in my abilities.
I listen to my inner wisdom.
I am tough and durable.

I can do anything.
I am completely unlimited.
I only think about the things I want to happen.
I am honest.
I am forgiving.
I am trustworthy.
I am very responsible.
I take care of my responsibilities.
I am wealthy.
I am prosperous.
I am abundant.
I am divinely protected.
I think big.
I believe in myself and my abilities.
I am extremely confident.
I have the courage to by myself.
I love me.
I am a bright student.
I value my education.
Obtaining knowledge is very important to me.
I love and value my family.
I go after what I want and I accomplish my goals.
I am a go getter.
My thoughts are very powerful and I choose them carefully.
I am brilliant wise and wonderful.
I love myself deeply.

I believe in my ability to succeed.
I am smart.
I am brilliant.
I am intelligent.
I am a fast learner.
Learning is fun and exciting.
I read write and learn very quickly.
I have many gifts and talents.
I make wise decisions.
I enjoy eating healthy foods.
I am destined to live a life of prosperity.
My thoughts create my world.
All is well in my world.
I think positive thus creating a positive world.
My positive attitude attracts positive situations and positive circumstances.
What I think about often eventually becomes my reality.
I attract situations that matches how I feel.
I visualize what I want often.
I talk about what I want often.
I think about what I want often.
I am a kind and generous person.
I show compassion towards others.
I treat people how I want to be treated.
What I do to others I actually do to myself.
I take my schoolwork very seriously.

I am dedicated to being a wonderful student.
There isn't anything that I cannot be do or have.
I excel in my academics.
I am a natural born leader.
I am strong fit and athletic.
My mind is powerful.
I use it wisely.
I am safe.
I am loved.
I am friendly.
I am brave.
I am courageous.
I am a winner.
I am very creative.

I believe in myself.
I trust in my abilities.
I am confident.
I make friends easily.
I am a good person.
I am a good friend.
I always overcome my challenges.
I believe in my abilities.
I listen to my inner wisdom.
I am tough and durable.

I can do anything.
I am completely unlimited.
I only think about things I want to happen.
I am honest.
I am forgiving.
I am trustworthy.
I am very responsible.
I take care of my responsibilities.
I am wealthy.
I am prosperous.
I am abundant.
I am divinely protected.
I think big.
I believe in myself and my abilities.
I am extremely confident.
I have the courage to by myself.
I love me.
I am a bright student.
I value my education.
Obtaining knowledge is very important to me.
I love and value my family.
I go after what I want and I accomplish my goals.
I am a go getter.
My thoughts are very powerful and I choose them carefully.
I am brilliant wise and wonderful.
I love myself deeply.

I believe in my ability to succeed.
I am smart.
I am brilliant.
I am intelligent.
I am a fast learner.
Learning is fun and exciting.
I read, write and learn very quickly.
I have many gifts and talents.
I make wise decisions.
I enjoy eating healthy foods.
I am destined to live a life of prosperity.
My thoughts create my world.
All is well in my world.
I think positive thus creating a positive world.
My positive attitude attracts positive situations and positive circumstances.
What I think about often eventually becomes my reality.
I attract situations that matches how I feel.
I visualize what I want often.
I talk about what I want often.
I think about what I want often.
I am a kind and generous person.
I show compassion towards others.
I treat people how I want to be treated.
What I do to others I actually do myself.
I take my schoolwork very seriously.

I am dedicated to being a wonderful student.
There isn't anything that I cannot be do or have.
I excel in my academics.
I am a natural born leader.
I am strong fit and athletic.
My mind is powerful and I use it wisely.
I am safe.
I am loved.
I am friendly.
I am brave.
I am courageous.
I am a winner.
I am very creative.
I believe in myself.
I trust my abilities.
I am confident.
I make friends easily.
I am a good person.
I am a good friend.
I always overcome my challenges.
I believe in my abilities.
I listen to my inner wisdom.
I am tough and durable.
I can do anything.
I am completely unlimited.
I only think about the things I want to happen.
I am honest.

I am forgiving.
I am trustworthy.
I am very responsible.
I take care of my responsibilities.
I am wealthy.
I am prosperous.
I am abundant.
I am divinely protected.
I think big.
I believe in myself and my abilities.
I am extremely confident.

I have the courage to by myself.
I love me.
I am a bright student.
I value my education.
Obtaining knowledge is very important to me.
I love and value my family.
I go after what I want and I accomplish my goals.
I am a go getter.

My thoughts are very powerful and I choose them carefully.

I am brilliant wise and wonderful.
I love myself deeply.
I believe in my ability to succeed.
I am smart.
I am brilliant.
I am intelligent.
I am a fast learner.
Learning is fun and exciting.
I read, write and learn very quickly.
I have many gifts and talents.
I make wise decisions.
I enjoy eating healthy foods.
I am destined to live a life of prosperity.
My thoughts create my world.
All is well in my world.
I think positive thus creating a positive world.
My positive attitude attracts positive situations and positive circumstances.
What I think about often eventually becomes my reality.
I attract situations that matches how I feel.
I visualize what I want often.
I talk about what I want often.
I think about what I want often.
I am a kind and generous person.
I show compassion towards others.
I treat people how I want to be treated.

What I do to others I actually do to myself.
I take my schoolwork very seriously.
I am dedicated to being a wonderful student.
There isn't anything that I cannot be do or have.
I excel in my academics.
I am a natural born leader.
I am strong fit and athletic.
My mind is powerful.
I use it wisely.
I am safe.
I am loved.
I am friendly.
I am brave.
I am courageous.
I am a winner.
I am very creative.

I believe in myself.
I trust in my abilities.
I am confident.
I make friends easily.
I am a good person.
I am a good friend.
I always overcome my challenges.
I believe in my abilities.

I listen to my inner wisdom.
I am tough and durable.
I can do anything.
I am completely unlimited.
I only think about things I want to happen.
I am honest.
I am forgiving.
I am trustworthy.
I am very responsible.
I take care of my responsibilities.
I am wealthy.
I am prosperous.
I am abundant.
I am divinely protected.
I think big.
I believe in myself and my abilities.
I am extremely confident.
I have the courage to by myself.
I love me.
I am a bright student.
I value my education.
Obtaining knowledge is very important to me.
I love and value my family.
I go after what I want and I accomplish my goals.
I am a go getter.
My thoughts are very powerful and I choose them carefully.

I am brilliant wise and wonderful.
I love myself deeply.
I believe in my ability to succeed.
I am smart.
I am brilliant.
I am intelligent.
I am a fast learner.
Learning is fun and exciting.
I read write and learn very quickly.
I have many gifts and talents.
I make wise decisions.
I enjoy eating healthy foods.
I am destined to live a life of prosperity.
My thoughts create my world.
All is well in my world.
I think positive thus creating a positive world.
My positive attitude attracts positive situations and positive circumstances.
What I think about often eventually becomes my reality.
I attract situations that matches how I feel.
I visualize what I want often.
I talk about what I want often.
I think about what I want often.
I am a kind and generous person.
I show compassion towards others.
I treat people how I want to be treated.

What I do to others I actually do myself.
I take my schoolwork very seriously.
I am dedicated to being a wonderful student.
There isn't anything that I cannot be do or have.
I excel in my academics.
I am a natural born leader.
I am strong fit and athletic.
My mind is powerful and I use it wisely.
I am safe.
I am loved.
I am friendly.
I am brave.
I am courageous.
I am a winner.
I am very creative.
I believe in myself.
I trust my abilities.
I am confident.
I make friends easily.
I am a good person.
I am a good friend.
I always overcome my challenges.
I believe in my abilities.
I listen to my inner wisdom.
I am tough and durable.
I can do anything.
I am completely unlimited.

I only think about the things I want to happen.
I am honest.
I am forgiving.
I am trustworthy.
I am very responsible.
I take care of my responsibilities.
I am wealthy.
I am prosperous.
I am abundant.
I am divinely protected.
I think big.
I believe in myself and my abilities.
I am extremely confident.

I have the courage to by myself.
I love me.
I am a bright student.
I value my education.
Obtaining knowledge is very important to me.
I love and value my family.
I go after what I want and I accomplish my goals.
I am a go getter.

My thoughts are very powerful and I choose them carefully.
I am brilliant wise and wonderful.
I love myself deeply.
I believe in my ability to succeed.
I am smart.
I am brilliant.
I am intelligent.
I am a fast learner.
Learning is fun and exciting.
I read write and learn very quickly.
I have many gifts and talents.
I make wise decisions.
I enjoy eating healthy foods.
I am destined to live a life of prosperity.
My thoughts create my world.
All is well in my world.
I think positive thus creating a positive world.
My positive attitude attracts positive situations and positive circumstances.
What I think about often eventually becomes my reality.
I attract situations that matches how I feel.
I visualize what I want often.
I talk about what I want often.
I think about what I want often.
I am a kind and generous person.

I show compassion towards others.
I treat people how I want to be treated.
What I do to others I actually do to myself.
I take my schoolwork very seriously.
I am dedicated to being a wonderful student.
There isn't anything that I cannot be do or have.
I excel in my academics.
I am a natural born leader.
I am strong fit and athletic.
My mind is powerful.
I use it wisely.
I am safe.
I am loved.
I am friendly.
I am brave.
I am courageous.
I am a winner.
I am very creative.

I believe in myself.
I trust in my abilities.
I am confident.
I make friends easily.
I am a good person.
I am a good friend.

I always overcome my challenges.
I believe in my abilities.
I listen to my inner wisdom.
I am tough and durable.
I can do anything.
I am completely unlimited.
I only think about things I want to happen.
I am honest.
I am forgiving.
I am trustworthy.
I am very responsible.
I take care of my responsibilities.
I am wealthy.
I am prosperous.
I am abundant.
I am divinely protected.
I think big.
I believe in myself and my abilities.
I am extremely confident.
I have the courage to by myself.
I love me.
I am a bright student.
I value my education.
Obtaining knowledge is very important to me.
I love and value my family.
I go after what I want and I accomplish my goals.
I am a go getter.

My thoughts are very powerful and I choose them carefully.
I am brilliant wise and wonderful.
I love myself deeply.
I believe in my ability to succeed.
I am smart.
I am brilliant.
I am intelligent.
I am a fast learner.
Learning is fun and exciting.
I read write and learn very quickly.
I have many gifts and talents.
I make wise decisions.
I enjoy eating healthy foods.
I am destined to live a life of prosperity.
My thoughts create my world.
All is well in my world.
I think positive thus creating a positive world.
My positive attitude attracts positive situations and positive circumstances.
What I think about often eventually becomes my reality.
I attract situations that matches how I feel.
I visualize what I want often.
I talk about what I want often.
I think about what I want often.
I am a kind and generous person.

I show compassion towards others.
I treat people how I want to be treated.
What I do to others I actually do myself.
I take my schoolwork very seriously.
I am dedicated to being a wonderful student.
There isn't anything that I cannot be do or have.
I excel in my academics.
I am a natural born leader.
I am strong fit and athletic.
My mind is powerful and I use it wisely.
I am safe.
I am loved.
I am friendly.
I am brave.
I am courageous.
I am a winner.
I am very creative.
I believe in myself.
I trust my abilities.
I am confident.
I make friends easily.
I am a good person.
I am a good friend.
I always overcome my challenges.
I believe in my abilities.
I listen to my inner wisdom.
I am tough and durable.

I can do anything.
I am completely unlimited.
I only think about the things I want to happen.
I am honest.
I am forgiving.
I am trustworthy.
I am very responsible.
I take care of my responsibilities.
I am wealthy.
I am prosperous.
I am abundant.
I am divinely protected.
I think big.
I believe in myself and my abilities.
I am extremely confident.

I have the courage to by myself.
I love me.
I am a bright student.
I value my education.
Obtaining knowledge is very important to me.
I love and value my family.
I go after what I want and I accomplish my goals.
I am a go getter.

My thoughts are very powerful and I choose them carefully.
I am brilliant wise and wonderful.
I love myself deeply.
I believe in my ability to succeed.
I am smart.
I am brilliant.
I am intelligent.
I am a fast learner.
Learning is fun and exciting.
I read write and learn very quickly.
I have many gifts and talents.
I make wise decisions.
I enjoy eating healthy foods.
I am destined to live a life of prosperity.
My thoughts create my world.
All is well in my world.
I think positive thus creating a positive world.
My positive attitude attracts positive situations and positive circumstances.
What I think about often eventually becomes my reality.
I attract situations that matches how I feel.
I visualize what I want often.
I talk about what I want often.
I think about what I want often.
I am a kind and generous person.

I show compassion towards others.
I treat people how I want to be treated.
What I do to others I actually do to myself.
I take my schoolwork very seriously.
I am dedicated to being a wonderful student.
There isn't anything that I cannot be do or have.
I excel in my academics.
I am a natural born leader.
I am strong fit and athletic.
My mind is powerful.
I use it wisely.
I am safe.
I am loved.
I am friendly.
I am brave.
I am courageous.
I am a winner.
I am very creative.

I believe in myself.
I trust in my abilities.
I am confident.
I make friends easily.
I am a good person.
I am a good friend.

I always overcome my challenges.
I believe in my abilities.
I listen to my inner wisdom.
I am tough and durable.
I can do anything.
I am completely unlimited.
I only think about things I want to happen.
I am honest.
I am forgiving.
I am trustworthy.
I am very responsible.
I take care of my responsibilities.
I am wealthy.
I am prosperous.
I am abundant.
I am divinely protected.
I think big.
I believe in myself and my abilities.
I am extremely confident.
I have the courage to by myself.
I love me.
I am a bright student.
I value my education.
Obtaining knowledge is very important to me.
I love and value my family.
I go after what I want and I accomplish my goals.
I am a go getter.

My thoughts are very powerful and I choose them carefully.
I am brilliant wise and wonderful.
I love myself deeply.
I believe in my ability to succeed.
I am smart.
I am brilliant.
I am intelligent.
I am a fast learner.
Learning is fun and exciting.
I read write and learn very quickly.
I have many gifts and talents.
I make wise decisions.
I enjoy eating healthy foods.
I am destined to live a life of prosperity.
My thoughts create my world.
All is well in my world.
I think positive thus creating a positive world.
My positive attitude attracts positive situations and positive circumstances.
What I think about often eventually becomes my reality.
I attract situations that matches how I feel.
I visualize what I want often.
I talk about what I want often.
I think about what I want often.
I am a kind and generous person.

I show compassion towards others.
I treat people how I want to be treated.
What I do to others I actually do myself.
I take my schoolwork very seriously.
I am dedicated to being a wonderful student.
There isn't anything that I cannot be do or have.
I excel in my academics.
I am a natural born leader.
I am strong fit and athletic.
My mind is powerful and I use it wisely.
I am safe.
I am loved.
I am friendly.
I am brave.
I am courageous.
I am a winner.
I am very creative.
I believe in myself.
I trust my abilities.
I am confident.
I make friends easily.
I am a good person.
I am a good friend.
I always overcome my challenges.
I believe in my abilities.
I listen to my inner wisdom.
I am tough and durable.

I can do anything.
I am completely unlimited.
I only think about the things I want to happen.
I am honest.
I am forgiving.
I am trustworthy.
I am very responsible.
I take care of my responsibilities.
I am wealthy.
I am prosperous.
I am abundant.
I am divinely protected.
I think big.
I believe in myself and my abilities.
I am extremely confident.

I have the courage to by myself.
I love me.
I am a bright student.
I value my education.
Obtaining knowledge is very important to me.
I love and value my family.
I go after what I want and I accomplish my goals.
I am a go getter.

My thoughts are very powerful and I choose them carefully.
I am brilliant wise and wonderful.
I love myself deeply.
I believe in my ability to succeed.
I am smart.
I am brilliant.
I am intelligent.
I am a fast learner.
Learning is fun and exciting.
I read write and learn very quickly.
I have many gifts and talents.
I make wise decisions.
I enjoy eating healthy foods.
I am destined to live a life of prosperity.
My thoughts create my world.
All is well in my world.
I think positive thus creating a positive world.
My positive attitude attracts positive situations and positive circumstances.
What I think about often eventually becomes my reality.
I attract situations that matches how I feel.
I visualize what I want often.
I talk about what I want often.
I think about what I want often.
I am a kind and generous person.

I show compassion towards others.
I treat people how I want to be treated.
What I do to others I actually do to myself.
I take my schoolwork very seriously.
I am dedicated to being a wonderful student.
There isn't anything that I cannot be do or have.
I excel in my academics.
I am a natural born leader.
I am strong fit and athletic.
My mind is powerful.
I use it wisely.
I am safe.
I am loved.
I am friendly.
I am brave.
I am courageous.
I am a winner.
I am very creative.

I believe in myself.
I trust in my abilities.
I am confident.
I make friends easily.
I am a good person.
I am a good friend.

I always overcome my challenges.
I believe in my abilities.
I listen to my inner wisdom.
I am tough and durable.
I can do anything.
I am completely unlimited.
I only think about things I want to happen.
I am honest.
I am forgiving.
I am trustworthy.
I am very responsible.
I take care of my responsibilities.
I am wealthy.
I am prosperous.
I am abundant.
I am divinely protected.
I think big.
I believe in myself and my abilities.
I am extremely confident.
I have the courage to by myself.
I love me.
I am a bright student.
I value my education.
Obtaining knowledge is very important to me.
I love and value my family.
I go after what I want and I accomplish my goals.
I am a go getter.

My thoughts are very powerful and I choose them carefully.
I am brilliant wise and wonderful.
I love myself deeply.
I believe in my ability to succeed.
I am smart.
I am brilliant.
I am intelligent.
I am a fast learner.
Learning is fun and exciting.
I read write and learn very quickly.
I have many gifts and talents.
I make wise decisions.
I enjoy eating healthy foods.
I am destined to live a life of prosperity.
My thoughts create my world.
All is well in my world.
I think positive thus creating a positive world.
My positive attitude attracts positive situations and positive circumstances.
What I think about often eventually becomes my reality.
I attract situations that matches how I feel.
I visualize what I want often.
I talk about what I want often.
I think about what I want often.
I am a kind and generous person.

I show compassion towards others.
I treat people how I want to be treated.
What I do to others I actually do myself.
I take my schoolwork very seriously.
I am dedicated to being a wonderful student.
There isn't anything that I cannot be do or have.
I excel in my academics.
I am a natural born leader.
I am strong fit and athletic.
My mind is powerful and I use it wisely.
I am safe.
I am loved.
I am friendly.
I am brave.
I am courageous.
I am a winner.
I am very creative.
I believe in myself.
I trust my abilities.
I am confident.
I make friends easily.
I am a good person.
I am a good friend.
I always overcome my challenges.
I believe in my abilities.
I listen to my inner wisdom.
I am tough and durable.

I can do anything.
I am completely unlimited.
I only think about the things I want to happen.
I am honest.
I am forgiving.
I am trustworthy.
I am very responsible.
I take care of my responsibilities.
I am wealthy.
I am prosperous.
I am abundant.
I am divinely protected.
I think big.
I believe in myself and my abilities.
I am extremely confident.

I have the courage to by myself.
I love me.
I am a bright student.
I value my education.
Obtaining knowledge is very important to me.
I love and value my family.
I go after what I want and I accomplish my goals.
I am a go getter.

My thoughts are very powerful and I choose them carefully.
I am brilliant wise and wonderful.
I love myself deeply.
I believe in my ability to succeed.
I am smart.
I am brilliant.
I am intelligent.
I am a fast learner.
Learning is fun and exciting.
I read write and learn very quickly.
I have many gifts and talents.
I make wise decisions.
I enjoy eating healthy foods.
I am destined to live a life of prosperity.
My thoughts create my world.
All is well in my world.
I think positive thus creating a positive world.
My positive attitude attracts positive situations and positive circumstances.
What I think about often eventually becomes my reality.
I attract situations that matches how I feel.
I visualize what I want often.
I talk about what I want often.
I think about what I want often.
I am a kind and generous person.

I show compassion towards others.
I treat people how I want to be treated.
What I do to others I actually do to myself.
I take my schoolwork very seriously.
I am dedicated to being a wonderful student.
There isn't anything that I cannot be do or have.
I excel in my academics.
I am a natural born leader.
I am strong fit and athletic.
My mind is powerful.
I use it wisely.
I am safe.
I am loved.
I am friendly.
I am brave.
I am courageous.
I am a winner.
I am very creative.

I believe in myself.
I trust in my abilities.
I am confident.
I make friends easily.
I am a good person.
I am a good friend.

I always overcome my challenges.
I believe in my abilities.
I listen to my inner wisdom.
I am tough and durable.
I can do anything.
I am completely unlimited.
I only think about things I want to happen.
I am honest.
I am forgiving.
I am trustworthy.
I am very responsible.
I take care of my responsibilities.
I am wealthy.
I am prosperous.
I am abundant.
I am divinely protected.
I think big.
I believe in myself and my abilities.
I am extremely confident.
I have the courage to by myself.
I love me.
I am a bright student.
I value my education.
Obtaining knowledge is very important to me.
I love and value my family.
I go after what I want and I accomplish my goals.
I am a go getter.

My thoughts are very powerful and I choose them carefully.
I am brilliant wise and wonderful.
I love myself deeply.
I believe in my ability to succeed.
I am smart.
I am brilliant.
I am intelligent.
I am a fast learner.
Learning is fun and exciting.
I read write and learn very quickly.
I have many gifts and talents.
I make wise decisions.
I enjoy eating healthy foods.
I am destined to live a life of prosperity.
My thoughts create my world.
All is well in my world.
I think positive thus creating a positive world.
My positive attitude attracts positive situations and positive circumstances.
What I think about often eventually becomes my reality.
I attract situations that matches how I feel.
I visualize what I want often.
I talk about what I want often.
I think about what I want often.
I am a kind and generous person.

I show compassion towards others.
I treat people how I want to be treated.
What I do to others I actually do myself.
I take my schoolwork very seriously.
I am dedicated to being a wonderful student.
There isn't anything that I cannot be do or have.
I excel in my academics.
I am a natural born leader.
I am strong fit and athletic.
My mind is powerful and I use it wisely.
I am safe.
I am loved.
I am friendly.
I am brave.
I am courageous.
I am a winner.
I am very creative.
I believe in myself.
I trust my abilities.
I am confident.
I make friends easily.
I am a good person.
I am a good friend.
I always overcome my challenges.
I believe in my abilities.
I listen to my inner wisdom.
I am tough and durable.

I can do anything.
I am completely unlimited.
I only think about the things I want to happen.
I am honest.
I am forgiving.
I am trustworthy.
I am very responsible.
I take care of my responsibilities.
I am wealthy.
I am prosperous.
I am abundant.
I am divinely protected.
I think big.
I believe in myself and my abilities.
I am extremely confident.

I have the courage to by myself.
I love me.
I am a bright student.
I value my education.
Obtaining knowledge is very important to me.
I love and value my family.
I go after what I want and I accomplish my goals.
I am a go getter.

My thoughts are very powerful and I choose them carefully.
I am safe.
I am loved.
I am friendly.
I am brave.

61 minutes

CONCLUSION

Thank you so much for listening to *Kids Bedtime Sleep Meditations.*

I hope this book has helped you have lots of wonderful dreams and amazing nights of sleep.

If you ever find yourself stressed out, angry, overwhelmed or sad, you can always refer to this book's teachings and re-listen to it again.

If you enjoyed this book and if it has helped you have a better night's sleep, be sure to leave a thoughtful review on Amazon of how this book has helped you. This is so more kids like you can have amazing sleeps every night!

Thank you again for listening to this book and I wish you all the love, happiness and amazing nights of sleep ahead!

KIDS BEDTIME MEDITATIONS FOR SLEEP

Guided Night Time Short Stories To Help Toddlers & Kids Fall Asleep At Night, Relax, And Have Beautiful Dreams

Author: Sleepy Willow

Do not listen to this audiobook while driving or operating machinery.

INTRODUCTION

Thank you for listening and choosing *Bedtime Meditations For Kids.*

In this magical and wonderful book, you will be taken on many adventures and listen to wonderful stories that will help you to fall asleep peacefully every night. I hope that you and your children will have hours of fun listening to these stories. Each story in this book will be entertaining and will have small lessons that your child can learn from. You will learn many skills that can help you relax your mind and body, so you have the most amazing sleep every night. Each story contains valuable lessons while relieving stress. Each story will empower you and your children to improve your self-confidence and self-esteem. You will learn how to deal with your emotions better and communicate them more effectively.

Children who experience lots of nightmares might be scared to fall asleep at night and might have a hard time relaxing at night because they are afraid of scary dreams. This book will help you combat and get rid of those fears. Each story will help you feel more relax, calm, loved and completely safe. You have nothing to worry about from now on.

After you have brushed your teeth, combed your hair and put on nice comfortable pajamas, it's time for you to snuggle down in bed and get ready for sleep. You can now pick any story to help you relax and drift off to an amazing sleep.

Make sure you listen to each story and follow along. Each story has a relaxing meditation to help you get cozy and comfortable for a good night's sleep.

Are you ready to begin your bedtime meditation stories? Choose any story to begin your adventure now!

CHAPTER 1

Sleepy Space Adventures

Are you ready for a special and magical adventure? This is an adventure where you will get to meet the Creator of Dreams.
Close your eyes and take a deep breath in through your nose.
Feel your tummy expand and breath out through your mouth.
Again take a deep breath in through your nose.
Feel your tummy expand like a balloon.
Now breathe out.
One last time big deep breath in and gently breathe out through your mouth.
Well done!
Now imagine a bubble flowing of pure white light.
This light surrounds your whole body, and this light is very bright.

It is almost a bluish color.
It is very soothing and very gentle to the touch.
This light is like a force field of protection.
This light only allows love and positivity to enter white you are away on your adventures.
Now imagine yourself in your bedroom tucked up nicely in your cozy bed.
You notice a twinkling light coming from your bedroom window.
You get up to investigate this light, and to your astonishment, there is a little small fairy tapping on your window sill.
She has a wand and has small tiny wings.
She is so beautiful to look at.
Can you see this magical fairy?

You open your bedroom window she smiles at you.
There is a magical glow around her, and you are absolutely in awe within her presence.
It is an extraordinary fairy.
She points her want up to the sky, and you notice a huge hole appearing in the night sky.
It is a hole with a giant eye peering out of it!
You have never seen anything like this before in your life although the eye looks very friendly and kind.
The fairy tells you there is no need to worry.

This is the eye of the Creator of Dreams.
You have been chosen to take a trip to meet this wonderful being.
He is the creator of all dreams and the creator of sweet lullabies.
They are both here to escort you to the kingdom.
The fairy says it is such a great honor to be chosen by the Creator of Dreams.
You have to be someone super special.
She tells you that the Creator of Dreams only communicates through your thoughts.
It is such a magnificent being, and it is very excited to meet you.

The fairy waves her magic wand and showers you with golden dust.
This golden dust gives you the ability to fly!
You will be flying to see the Creator of Dreams.
You glide in the air and can fully control what you are doing.
You keep going up and up.
What can you see below you?

You keep going higher and higher now.
The stars seem to be brighter and brighter.

Can you see them?
What else can you see?
Just take a few moments to enjoy flying in the air.
The fairy will always you following you wherever you go.
Maybe you find out more about her life.
You can tell her about yours.
Maybe you can learn just a little bit more about this Creator of Dreams.
Enjoy your journey with the fairy.

As you look ahead of you, you notice a huge slit in the sky where the giant eye was looking down.
Then you two just fly right through the little hole.
Wow!
You arrive in a truly wonderful and magical land.
You have never seen anything like this before.
Stardust and gold fills the air around you, and you see colors and beings that you have never seen before.
It is so alive.
You notice millions and millions of what looks like little glowing bubbles.
The fairy tells you that people's dreams are inside all of these bubbles and were created by the Creator of Dreams.

It is ready to be sent off to people all over the universe to help them all get a wonderful and good night's sleep.

Can you see these magical and beautiful bubbles?

Spend a little time while looking around at the amazing kingdom of the Creator of Dreams with your beautiful little fairy friend.

Maybe you can enter some of the dream bubbles with your fairy by your side.

See what adventures you could go on.

Maybe you could even enter one of the empty dream bubbles and create a dream of your own.

Oh, how wonderful that would be.

If you have any questions, you can ask the magic fairy.

You can ask them anything you want.

Just enjoy your time here.

Did you enjoy your time wandering the kingdom of the Creator of Dreams?

Did you enter any of the dream bubbles?

Or did you create any of your very own dreams?

You now look ahead of you, and you notice a massive being sitting cross-legged on a golden white cloud made out of fairy dust.

You know that in your heart, this must be the Creator of Dreams.

You feel so happy, so safe, and so protected in the company of this wonderful being called the Creator of Dreams.

The Creator of Dreams seems to be very happy to see you.

He beckons you up onto the golden fairy dust cloud.

It is very high because the Creator of Dreams is huge.

The Creator of Dreams stretches out his hand, and you step onto it.

He lifts you up and has you standing in his giant hand.

Take a few moments and chat with the Creator of Dreams before he sings his goodnight lullaby.

Ask him anything you would like.

Anything at all.

The Creator of Dreams now gently puts you down next to the fairy.

Every being in the kingdom suddenly stops and becomes very still and totally quiet.
The fairy whispers to you that he is about to sing the goodnight lullaby.
This lullaby helps to sent sweet dreams to everyone in the universe.
This lullaby helps everyone to fall asleep.

You are now feeling a little tired yourself.
Listen very closely.
Close your eyes.
Leave your thoughts away until tomorrow.
You are safe.
You are protected.
So just dream.
I am the Creator of Dreams here to make your dreams come true.
So Dream Dream Dream.
Dream Dream Dream.

Oh, what a lovely and soothing song.
You are feeling very tired now yourself.

The Creator of Dreams points to a dream bubble with a wonderful and beautiful comfy-looking bed with huge pillows and a warm glowing night light.

You can enter this dream bubble and get some rest if you want.

Or maybe you can have some more dreams and more adventures around the kingdom.

Whenever you want to return home, the fairy will take you back.

Maybe you can even fall asleep with the fairy if you are tired.

Your eyes are becoming so tired now.

When you wake up in the morning, you will be right back in your bed, feeling very refreshed, filled with positivity, and so excited for the next trip to see the Creator of Dreams.

Good night and sleep tight.

Now imagine that you now find yourself at the beginning of a very long platform.

This platform is sort of looks like a train platform but so much bigger.

You see a sign saying The Galaxy Tour To The Sleepy Planets.

You never heard of this tour before, but you wonder what it could be.

You set off down the very long platform.

As you walk, you see mist and smoke in the distance.

The mist and smoke is floating and puffy.

You get nearer to the end of the platform, and you see something sticking out of the smoke.

It looks like a rocket or maybe even a ship.

You look closer, and it is a spaceship!

You notice a little desk next to you.

You did not notice it before but at the desk is a little man wearing a big spacesuit.

He is wearing a glass helmet and asks you for the ticket aboard this spaceship.

You explain to him that you do not have a ticket, and you look a bit puzzled.

He says, well, just try and check your pockets.

You reach in your pocket, and to your amazement, you pull out a ticket!

This ticket is big and golden.

You hand it to the man, and he steps away from the desk and asks you to follow him.

You two both go up a large flight of stairs.

As you go up the stairs, you start to see the spaceship even more.

It is super shiny and has giant massive rockets attached to the spaceship.

The spaceship is actually the thing that is producing all of the smoke you saw earlier.

This spaceship has lots of windows all around the top of the ship.

If you stand inside, you could probably see all around you.

Once you get to the top of the stairs, you step onto a metal platform.

This platform leads you to the door of the spaceship.

The man tells you to step inside and hands you your very own spacesuit.

You put it on, and then the two of you step into the cockpit of this spaceship.

You put your seatbelt on, and you see so many different colors, buttons, dials, and lights flashing everywhere.

This man in the spacesuit will be your guide on this magical trip.

You notice there is a big blue button.

You reach out to press the button, but the man says, "whoa whoa there! Do not touch that button! We are not ready yet."

He explains this is the sleep countdown button, and you can only press it until the button glows with color.

You want to press this button so bad, but you do not.

You have to listen to the guide.

Your guide tells you that we will be stopping at different planets.

These planets are all ones that are the best for sleeping.

You may even pick up some other travelers.

He is starting the countdown now.

You hear him counting down saying,

"Ten.

Nine.

Eight.

Seven."

You are getting so excited.

"Six.

Five.

Four.

Three."

You check your helmet is on properly.

"Two.

One.

Blast Off!"

Your spaceship starts to shake and rumble.

The noise coming from the engine of the ship is very, very loud now.

It is so loud your teeth and body start to rattle.

The massive spaceship lifts off, and with a massive whoosh, you find yourself already traveling so fast in the sky!

Now you are just starting to see stars and space.
You have just gone through the Earth's atmosphere.
You have now just entered space.
You are surrounded by the most beautiful sparkling stars.
You can see amazing planets around you.
You feel so peaceful.
You feel so relaxed just floating among the stars.
You are just floating in space inside a great big spaceship.
The loud engines are quiet now.
It is so peaceful, just drifting among the stars.
You look out of the window, and you see shiny little moon rocks fly past all around you.
These rocks are glowing.
You also see comets streaking past the sky.
You can see the shiny trails the comets leave.
You can even see small and large meteorites.
You also catch a glimpse of a shooting star.
It looks so wonderful.
Now you can even see some other spaceships floating past you.
You wonder where they are going.
You see so many other things that you have never seen before.
You see Saturn and its large rings.
You can see the planet Uranus as you fly past it.

You even ply past Neptune.
Wow, everything in space is so beautiful.
There are so many planets in space, and each one is beautiful in its own way.
But you look back, and you see Earth.
Earth is definitely the most beautiful of them all.

You are starting to feel a bit sleepy now.
Although you are still very excited about your adventure ahead.
Your guide takes the spaceship up even higher.
You notice a massive planet, and it is purple colored.
This planet is the Purple Snuggle Planet.
Your guide tells you this planet is made from only lavender.
Only lavender grows there, and that on a good day, you can even smell the lavender from inside the spaceship.

You fly towards another planet, and this one is shaped like a giant sofa.
It has big fluffy pillows, and you wonder what it would like to be on that planet.

Then the spaceship slowly flies past another planet, and there are so many of these sleepy planets.

Then on the final planet, you see so many people snuggled up into big fluffy blankets, and they are asleep in their beds.

You can see little tiny lights all switched off.

Then your guide tells you that this is the end of the tour.

He is now going to start the countdown for the most perfect night sleep you have ever had.

He reaches over, and he presses on the big blue button.

This starts the countdown.

Five.

You feel so very tired and sleepy.

So very very sleepy.

Four.

Your whole body is perfectly calm, relaxed and ready for the perfect sleep.

Three.

Your eyes are very heavy now and you close them for a little while.

Two.

You imagine that all the thoughts in your head are just dissolving away.

One.

Your eyes are finally closed and you slowly drift off into sleep.

The spaceship gently slows down and just floats peacefully.
That stars are twinkling.
Soon you will be deeply asleep.
You will be off on a wonderful journey to the most amazing peaceful sleep.
It will carry you all the way through the morning but always remember you are completely safe and loved.
You are always protected.

Now imagine yourself inside a big shiny spaceship.
You are wearing a brilliant white spacesuit.
Now take a seat and fasten your seatbelt.
Get ready for a big adventure.
You are now going to zoom off into outer space.
Let the countdown begin.
Ten.
Nine.
Eight.
Seven.
Six.
Five.
Four.
Three.

Two.
One.
Blast Off!
You go shooting up into the sky.
You keep going higher and higher.
You have never been this high before!
You are so excited.
You are in your very own spaceship, and you are the one controlling it!
Wow! This rocket ship is so fast!
Now you have arrived in space.
You feel so free and wonderful.
You look out of your window and you see planet Earth behind you.
It looks so beautiful from up here.
Can you see it?

Can you see how blue and beautiful the earth is?
Hey look, can you see your home?

As you look around in space, you can also see thousands and thousands of stars all shining brightly.

Are you able to see other planets?
Or even are you able to see other galaxies?
Have a good look around you.
See if there is anything else you can see.
You feel so safe and so happy.
You feel amazing just looking at the stars shining brightly.
Can you see the moon?

You have now spotted the moon.
You start heading straight towards it.
You bring your spaceship down and land on the surface of the moon.
You want to go outside and explore the moon.
You are so fascinated.
You make sure your helmet is on tightly.
You open the door and have a step outside.
Your feet barely touches the ground.
You find yourself bouncing all along the surface.
Remember the gravity is not as strong here, so you can float away in space if you are not careful.
You feel so light and weightless.
You feel like you could almost just float away.
You are just laughing and having so much fun now.
You feel so happy here on the moon.

It is like every time you bounce, your worries just seem to melt away.
You feel so safe, so calm and very, very carefree and happy.
Stay here a little while longer and enjoy yourself.
Take sometime to explore the rest of the moon.
Have a good look around.
See if you can find any aliens on this moon or even a spaceman or spacewoman to talk to.
Can you see anyone?
Look at those rocks.
Are you able to tell what kind of rock that is?
What color are they?
Go have some fun looking around this truly amazing place.

Now it is time for you to return home.
It is time to return back to your spaceship.
You jump in and sit in the cockpit.
You fasten your seatbelt and start the countdown again.
Ten.
Nine.
Eight.
Seven.

Six.
Five.
Four.
Three.
Two.
One.
Blast Off!
You blast off into space and go shooting up away from the moon.
You are starting to pass the stars and you feel amazing.
You feel happy and so free.
You look around you and out your window.
You see the moon far behind you now, just getting smaller and smaller.
It only takes you a few minutes to arrive back home.
You feel so happy.
You had the most amazing adventure tonight.
You went to the moon and bounced and had the time of your life.

Now imagine in your peaceful mind that hanging from your wardrobe is a special pair of pajamas.
These pajamas have pictures and designs of moons, stars, spaceships, and planets all over it.
What color are these pajamas?

Can you see it?

You take them out of your wardrobe and put them on.

You suddenly find yourself instantly transported up in the night sky.

These special pajamas have taken you all the way up into the clouds!

They keep taking you higher and higher.

They take you soaring through the clouds.

You see the moon shining and glowing very brightly above you.

It looks so beautiful, so warm and so comforting.

Your pajamas still take you higher and higher.

Suddenly, you realize that you are now flying in space.

Wow! These pajamas are the best!

This is so much fun!

You feel so relaxed, so peaceful, and so calm.

You are just floating through space, just drifting along.

You are just drifting along with no particular place to be.

As you float around, you see all different kinds of things.

You see comets whizzing past you.

You see the tails of these comets leaving a beautiful golden streak behind them.

You can see the asteroid belt.

You can even see all the planets in our solar system in the distance.

You wonder if there is anyone living on these planets.

You can see other galaxies and it looks so beautiful.

It is so dazzling to your eyes.

You look around with such amazement.

It is a light show. A wonderful display of light just for you.

As you float along in space, you notice something coming towards you.

What could it be?

As it gets closer, you realize it is a floating bed.

This bed is just floating along in space.

This is actually a very big and beautiful bed.

It has the fluffiest pillows and the softest blankets.

It is so inviting for you to just lay on it.

Go and try it.

Try and lay on this beautiful bed.

You move closer to the bed and you climb up onto it.

Once you get on you feel deeply relaxed.

You feel so sage and so comfortable.

You get under the covers and you snuggle yourself down deeper and deeper.

You put your head on the fluffy pillows and it feels so warm, so peaceful.

You can feel the bed rocking like a boat.
It is so soothing rocking from side to side.
You feel your whole body just wanting to just drift off into sleep.
You are laying here just drifting through space.
Space has its own relaxing vibe.
It is as space is singing you a sweet lullaby just for you.
You float through space so peacefully on your big bed.
You watch the comets as they fly by.
You see shooting stars granting you luck and happiness.
Your big beautiful bed is still rocking from side to side.

You feel so sleepy, so peaceful and so calm.
You feel so very relaxed and so safe.
You notice that the stars have gone out and not shining.
It is telling you it is time for sleep and is nighttime.
It is as if they are helping you fall into the best night's sleep you have ever had in your life.
Space is singing a special lullaby just for you.
It is gently nudging you into the perfect sleep in the world.

Your eyes are feeling so heavy now.
You feel so very sleepy.
You feel so peaceful.
Your whole body just feels soft and loose.
I think your body has already gone to sleep.
Just as you are about to drift off, you look down at your very special pajamas.
You smile happily to yourself really happy and please that you found these special pajamas in your wardrobe.
You are so thankful and happy you experienced this wonderful time in space.
Close your eyes and just rest now.
You are going to have the best night's sleep ever.

CHAPTER 2

Monster and Alien Friends

Make yourself all nice, comfortable and cozy in your bed.
Close your eyes and take a deep breath in.
Now slowly and gently let go of your breath.
Again deep breath in.
Then slowly and gently let your breath out.
One more time deep breath in.
And slowly and gently let your breath out.

Imagine you are surrounded by a beautiful white light.
This light is so bright.
This light is very pure and is a light of protection and peace.

Breathe in this pure white light.
Feel it as it enters your body.
It makes you feel completely warm and so very very safe.
Now imagine you are in a beautiful and lush green forest.
This forest has some of the most amazing trees you have ever seen.
Some of these trees are very tall and some are a little small.
Some of them even look like they are touching the sun since they are so tall.
You are standing on a very wide path deep in this forest.
It is a beautiful and sunny day.
The birds are chirping high above the trees.
You can hear tiny animals scurrying around, but you can't see them because they are moving so very fast.
You begin to walk and after a while, you see a cave up ahead of you.
You almost did not see it because it was surrounded by bushes.
As you talk about it, you think it would be an amazing idea to explore the cave.
You want to find out if there is anything in there.
You are not afraid.
In fact, you are actually really excited.

From the outside, the cave looks pretty dark, but you are not afraid of that either.
You notice a shimmering light all the way back in the cave.
It is a very big cave.
This cave looks so warm, so cozy, and very inviting to go into.
You wonder why there is a light in there, so you start to look at what this light is.
It is in the back of this very large room, and you see that this light is actually a burning torch.
You take the torch off of the wall and enter the second room.
You see something quite amazing.
It looks like someone actually lives in this room.
There is a small fire burning in the fireplace.
There is a table with lots of fruit on it.
In the middle of the table is a large bowl.
There is also a very large sofa full of colorful cushions.
It looks so cozy, and you wonder who on Earth lives here in a cave in the middle of the forest?
Suddenly you hear movement coming from the other rooms in the cave.
You wonder who it is.
Coming through the doorway is a very large being with a big smile on his face.

You think to yourself, oh my, I just walked into someone else's home!
Maybe they are upset.
Although the big friendly face greets you and says hello, I see you have come for a visit.
You take a closer look and it is just a great big friendly monster.
He does not look scary one bit.
In fact, he looks rather nice and always has a great big smile on his face and looks so happy.
He is very big and looks very squishy too.
He is a bluish greenish color with big ears.
You look into his eyes and they look so very kind.
The monster asks if you would like to stay and sit for a nice drink of lemonade.
Oh yes please!
I love lemonade.
The big monster says his name is Anthony.
He lives here in the cave all by himself.
He tells you he is so very happy you have come to visit him.
He does not get many people to come to see him and is very excited.
As you look around the room, you notice there are lots of pictures everywhere.
These pictures are of a very happy family.
Anthony tells you that this is his family and they live very far away.

He tells you that he doesn't get to see them very often.
Anthony hands you a very big glass of lemonade.
He tells you about his life and that he is very lonely.
He tells you that since he looks so different from everybody else and being so big, people are afraid of him.
Some people even think he is ugly just because he looks different.
This makes him very sad.
You say that he looks beautiful just the way he is and you would be happy that you are his friend.
Anthony is so happy that you are being so kind to him.
He asks if you can be best friends and you say, of course.
I would be very, very proud to have a friend like you.
For a little while longer, you and Anthony just sit and chat.
You tell each other about your lives.
You tell him where you go to school and all about school.
Anthony has never been to school, so he doesn't know what it is like.
For a little while longer just enjoy yourself with Anthony.
Just chat for a little while and get to know each other.

Now it is time for you to return home.

Before you go, Anthony asks if you would like to maybe have a sleepover.

You say oh yes please!

We can chat and hang out with each other for a lot longer.

Now Anthony shows you his bedroom and it is right next door.

It has two great big beds with such lovely soft blankets and pillows.

Anthony says you can choose whichever bed you like the best.

Anthony climbs up on his bed now and you two begin to chat some more.

There is so much for you two to talk about.

You can just talk and talk and talk until you both fall asleep.

You are so happy you have found a new best friend.

Anthony is so kind, gentle and his smile lights up the sky.

The two of you are feeling very sleepy now.

You both want to keep on chatting, but that is okay.

That is great, but you both want to sleep as well.

Whenever you both are ready, you say goodnight to each other, snuggle down and you will gently fall asleep.

Now imagine yourself sitting in the shade under a large tree.
This is a beautiful lush green tree, and you can see the branches reach so high up into the sky.
It looks as if this tree is trying to touch the sun.
It is as if they want to feel the warmth of the sun.
This lovely tree is filled with flowers of all different shapes and colors.
There are even a few baby rabbits playing and running around this tree.
These rabbits are just chasing each other and just having fun.

You see a very large sunflower further away in the beautiful meadow as you look around.
This sunflower has a spiral staircase running up the stem of this place.
You think wow I have never seen this before a very large sunflower with a staircase on it.
You notice that you cannot see the top of the flower because it is disappearing in the clouds.
Wow! This sunflower is really really big.
You stand up and decide to find out about this sunflower.
You decide you are going to climb the staircase to see where it leads to.

You are about to have a new adventure.
You reach the bottom of the sunflower and start to climb up it.
You climb, climb, climb and climb.
Your legs a starting to feel a little tired and a little worn out from all this exercise.
You feel like you want to give up and turn around, but you push through like a winner.
You need to keep climbing to reach the clouds.
You now have reached the clouds, and it feels like you are walking in a misty fog.
It feels very cool but still very determined to get to the top of the sunflower.
Then suddenly, your head pops out from the clouds.
You look around and you see an extraordinary but exciting land all around you.
There are fields of green and in these fields are the most gigantic trees you have ever seen.
These trees are like the size of mountains.
You climb off the sunflower and start to walk in these green fields.
You jump off the sunflower and disappear into the grass.
This grass is just not like any other grass but very huge grass.
It is so huge it is like you are walking through a forest.

You feel like you are a tiny insect.
The grass is so big and so tall.
The stem of the grass is also very thick and almost as thick as trees.

You begin to walk and see what you can find in this strange new land.
You wonder if there is anyone else here.
It is a little tough to walk around here because the ground is bumpy and not flat.
You keep slipping around.
After a while of walking, you see something gleaming up ahead of you.
You wonder what this could be and you catch a glimpse of something shiny in the sunlight.
As you get close to this shiny object, it gets bigger and bigger.
You are very unsure what this object is.
You notice that it is a spoon but a very giant and massive spoon.
Wow! This is a giant spoon the size of a ship!
Where on earth are you?
Who on earth would have giant spoons?
Who would even be able to pick these up?
Who would even be able to use them?

Suddenly a light flashes down above you.
You realize the only people who can use these are giants.
Maybe you are now in the land of giants.
You start to walk away from the spoon slowly, and you feel the ground begin to move and shake.
You fall over and you do not know what is causing this.
Is it an earthquake?
You see movement in the corner of your eye.
It is a dark shape lumbering towards you.
It is a giant bug.
You start running but you feel yourself being lifted into the air.
You go higher and higher and higher.
You are now moving very quickly through the air with something holding onto your back.
Then you are now placed down onto a large and safe rock away from the big bug.
You look into the eyes of a giant child.
You are a little scared but the child smiles at you and tells you not to be afraid.
You are not afraid of this child at all.
This kid giant is a young boy with a lovely smile.
He tells you that he rescued you from the big bug because he knew that he wanted you for dinner.
You thank him so much for his kindness and you tell him that you really did not want to get eaten.

The giant tells you that he reads stories all the time about humans and loves to read and listen to human fairy tales.

He asks if you like to see his home and all the toys he has.

You can immediately tell this giant is very kind and nice.

You say oh yes please!

He picks you up very gently and tells you that he will keep you safe no matter what.

The giant asks where you live and all about humans. He knows only stories that his parents have told him or what he has read in school.

He doesn't really believe all the fairytales.

For a few minutes, while he walks to his house, you talk to him and tell him all about humans.

You tell them how we live, you tell him about your family and you tell him about your school and friends.

You even tell him what you like to do on your free time and play.

Just talk with the friendly giant for a few minutes.

He is so nice and kind.

You arrive at the giant boys house.
You look around and you see that you are actually in his back garden.
The trees are the size of mountains, although they are normal-sized trees to the giant boy.
The giant boy shouts hello to his mom and then sneaks you up into his bedroom.
He gently places you on the floor and he sits down next to you.
There is a knock on his bedroom door and tells you to hide behind him.
He doesn't want his mom to see you.
You quickly run behind his back and the giant boy talks to his mom.
You look around his room and everything is so huge.
You see a pencil on his desk and it is the size of a street lamp.
There is a car toy and it is the size of a real car.
The bedroom door closes and the giant boy tells you to come back out.
His mom brought him a sandwich and offers you a piece of it.
This sandwich is the size of a bed!
It is so big!
The giant boy laughs and breaks off a little crumb for you.
This crumb is still the size of a basketball.

You say thank you because you were starting to get really hungry.
While you are eating this sandwich, the giant boy finally tells you his name.
His name is Jordan.
Jordan shows you his phone.
To no surprise, his phone is a giant one.
It is the size of a movie screen in the theaters.
For a little while, you and Jordan watch a little movie on his phone.
You both have a chat with each other about all the things you both love to do.
Jordan tells you all about his favorite movies he loves to watch.

Sadly the time has come.
It is time for you to go home.
Jordan takes you back outside and back to where the sunflower is.
This sunflower is still peeking out of the misty clouds.
He places you gently back on the sunflower and asks if you would ever like to come again.
You say yes of course because you had a wonderful time.
Also because you have made a new friend.

You never want to lose this friendship.
Jordan has been very kind to you and took such good care of you so you would not be hurt by anything.
This is what all friends should do.
Friends should help protect each other and help each other if they need it.
You smile and wave goodbye to Jordan.
You start climbing back down the spiral staircase around this beautiful sunflower.
You feel so so happy now.
Take a big deep breath in through your nose and gently breathe out through your mouth.
Again take a deep breath in and slowly and gently breathe out through your mouth.
One last time take a deep breath in and slowly and gently breathe out through your mouth.
Remember you can visit Jordan anytime you wish because Jordan is your new best friend.

Now imagine you are now in a beautiful meadow.
The sun is shining brightly and the birds are singing and chirping their beautiful songs.
You look around and see the most beautiful flowers of all different scents and colors.
Can you smell the flowers?
Can you see all the beautiful colors?

In the far distance, you catch a glimpse of a shiny object in the sky.

As you walk a little closer, it slowly gets bigger and bigger.

You suddenly realize that it is a UFO.

It looks like an alien spaceship.

It's like a flying saucer!

Wow, so amazing!

Can you see it as you walk closer?

As you get closer to the spaceship, you notice a little blue head pop out the top with a big huge happy smile on its face.

You think it is really funny and even start to laugh!

You have never seen something look like this.

He is only around one foot tall.

You are not scared of the alien at all.

In fact, it has one of the happiest and kindest face you have ever seen.

Is this alien a boy or a girl?

Take a good look at this lovely little happy blue alien.

What does this alien look like to you?

You are totally amazed.

Even though you do not know what this alien is saying because it speaks another language, you

somehow can understand every word that is being said.
What does the alien say to you?
Can you hear it?

The alien asks you if you want to ride on his spaceship?
You laugh and you say that I am too big!
Your ship is so small and tiny I could never fit in there.
Then suddenly, you magically just shrink down to the same size as the alien.
Wow! You can now get on board the ship!
How an earth did you do that?
The alien just used his special technology to make you tiny but don't worry he can return you to normal after.
You step into the ship and you see flashing lights everywhere.
You can hear buzzing and beeping everywhere.
Look around you.
What do you see?
What does the spaceship look like?

You feel rumbling and shaking beneath your feet.
The ship starts to move a little and then all of a sudden it takes off.
You sit down in the cockpit next to the blue alien.
You look outside the window of the spaceship and look at the earth behind you.
It is getting smaller and smaller.
What else can you see outside the window?

You are flying farther and farther away.
This spaceship is so fast!
You are enjoying the ride with your new blue alien friend so much!
For a little while, you two have a nice chat with each other.
You find out more about the aliens life.
Does he have a name?
Where does he come from?
Maybe he is on a super-secret mission for you.
Maybe they have a special gift to give you.
Enjoy the ride with this lovely alien.

The alien spaceship now lands safely back down in the beautiful meadow.

Wow, what an amazing journey you had with this blue alien!
The alien asks you if you two can do something before he leaves.
This is for the benefit of you, your family, everyone on earth, and for all of mankind.
The alien wants you to shine your light to send happiness, healing and love to planet Earth.
You can do this by imagining a breath of warm light coming from your heart.
See this white light as it grows bigger and bigger.
It comes out of your heart so big that it covers your entire body.
It is like a forcefield of light.
Fill this light with thoughts of love, happiness, peace and healing.
Send it to anyone who you think may need it.
It can be your friends, your family, an animal, or maybe just send it out to the whole wide world and let it shine so brightly down on everyone.
Send out the love.

You can send this white light to anyone that needs healing.
You can send it out whenever you like as well.

This service was for the blue alien and all life on this wonderful, amazing, beautiful planet we live on.
You notice the alien is already flying back home.
He also left a little note for you.
What does it say?

Now it is time for you to come home.
Take a deep breath in and slowly breathe out through your mouth.
Take another deep breath in and slowly breathe out through your mouth.

One more time, take a big deep breath in and slowly breathe out through your mouth.
Now imagine you are lying on your very own comfy bed.
You are all snuggled up and feeling nice and warm.
You notice something is lying on the floor.
What is it?
It's a book with a picture on it.
This picture is of the kindest and happiest alien you have ever seen in your life.
She looks so friendly and so nice.

You close your eyes and you wish with all your heart that you could meet her just once.
You smile and then open your eyes.
Now she is standing right in front of you!
She is smiling and waving at you!
You are absolutely shocked and amazed!
You can tell she is very kind and friendly.
She has the friendliest eyes and smile.

The little alien says hello so shyly.
You say hello back and look at her.
You see, she is very different from you.
She is a purplish color and has blue eyes.
She is wearing a yellow shirt with a bright yellow hat.
She even has yellow boots on.
She tells you her name is Indigo.
Wow, such an interesting name.
You invite her to have a seat on her bed and the two of you just chat.
She tells you where she comes from and how she got here.
For a few moments, just sit with Indigo and let you tell her about your life.
Tell her about your family.
You can maybe even introduce her to your family.
Just have a little chat with her and relax.

After a little while of talking to her, Indigo explains that she has a special kind of power.
Kind of like a superpower.
This superpower gives her the ability to take you to where she lives now.
Wouldn't that be so awesome and cool?
You can even have a sleepover on her planet if you would like to.
She explains that time does not exist where she lives.
You can then return home and no time will have passed by.
In fact, no one would even know that you are gone.
Wow this is so amazing and cool!
So of course you say yes.
How amazing is that?
Indigo tells you to close your eyes and open them again.
You do and in front of you, you see a swirling misty portal just going around and around.
Indigo takes your hand and tells you she will count to three and on three the two of you will jump.
Are you ready?
One, two, three, jump!
You two jump into the swirling mist.
It feels as though you are on a waterslide going around and around.

It is like you are sliding on a beautiful rainbow.
The colors are changing as you slide down.
Suddenly, you pop out of the mist and land with a little plop on some soft grass.
Well, it looks like grass, but you aren't really sure.
It looks green.
You look around and notice this planet is so amazingly beautiful.
There is so much color everywhere.
There are also all kinds of strange creatures walking around.
Some of them don't have eyes and some have many eyes.
They look so different compared to people on earth.
Although they all say hello to you with big kind smiles on their faces.
Wow, everyone is so friendly!
You think to yourself that this planet should be called the happy planet.
Everyone is so loving, friendly and nice.
Some creatures have many different colors and some are weird shaped.
Every creature goes out of their way to make you feel special and loved.
Wow this is the greatest planet ever.
For a little while, go and explore this wonderful planet.

Maybe you can visit all the cool things to do on this planet.
Maybe visit a park or go shopping.
See what they like to eat.
Visit the places that they live in.
See if your houses are the same.
Maybe even Indigo goes to school.
Maybe you can even go to an alien museum.
Maybe you can see a sporting event.
You decide what to do now.
Go and pick your favorite things.

Now you are feeling a bit sleepy after such an amazing day with Indigo.
She takes you back to her bedroom for the sleepover.
She shows you all around her amazing bedroom and all the toys she had in it.
She even has some action figures.
There are two hammocks in her bedroom.
One for you and one for her.
You climb into the hammock and it feels so comfortable and nice.
It is so relaxing and so calm.
This feels so nice after such a long and wonderful day.

You settle down into the cozy hammock and rock from side to side.
Wow this feels so peaceful.
This is so comfortable.
Indigo whispers goodnight to you and hopes you will have a wonderful sleep.
Close your eyes and gently sway from side to side in the hammock.
Just sway side to side.
Side to side.
When you wake up in the morning, you will be right back in your bed.
You know you can come here whenever you like.
Take a deep breath in and now slowly and gently breathe out.
You feel so relaxed and so happy.
Take another deep breath in and now slowly and gently breathe out.
Ahhh you feel so sleepy now.
Take another deep breath in and now slowly and gently breathe out.
Your eyes feel so tired.
Your breathing is soft and gentle now.
Every breath you take in will nourish all the positive thoughts and feelings.
You start to drift in and out of sleep now.
You are beginning to sink deeper and deeper into the soft lovely hammock.

You feel so peaceful.
You feel so happy.
You feel so safe and so very very loved.
Goodnight.
Sleep tight.

CHAPTER 3

Private Paradise

Close your eyes now and make yourself comfortable.
I want you to take a deep breath in through your nose.
Big deep breath in and gently and slowly breathe out through your mouth.
Again take a deep breath in through your nose and gently and slowly breathe out through your mouth.
One more time, deep breath in and slowly and gently breathe out through your mouth.
Now just bring your breathing back to its normal rhythm.
Feel your stomach and chest gently rise and fall.
You feel very peaceful.
You feel very calm.

You feel very relaxed.
With every breath you take, you can feel yourself becoming more and more relaxed.
You feel so at ease and happy.
You feel so peaceful.
You feel very very happy.
Your breathing is very light and almost still.
You are so relaxed now.
I want you to imagine yourself sitting in a large green field.
The sun is shining brightly, and it's such a beautiful clear day.
You can see for miles and miles.
You are very calm, very relaxed and very peaceful.
Can you hear the birds chirping and singing?
Can you hear the birds sing to each other?
Just sit here and take a good look around you.
What can you see?
What can you hear?
Can you see anybody else in this lovely field of yours?

As you sit here, when you have thoughts or feelings that you do not want to have, I want you to imagine a cloud floating past you.
You can have any shape and color of the cloud.

You just want the cloud to just rise up and drift away and away from you.
Let it drift away into the beautiful blue sky.

When the cloud is gone, wait for the next cloud to appear and just let these unwanted thoughts just float away with the cloud carrying those unwanted thoughts.
Don't think about these thoughts in the clouds just look at it as it passes you by.
Just watch it float away and even higher up into the beautiful blue sky.
If you have any other thoughts you want to let go of or do not like, then just place them inside the cloud and watch them float away.

Just watch the clouds as they pass in front of you.
Just let them go.
You can have different colored clouds.
Maybe a blue one, a red one, maybe a lovely yellow one.
You can see many different colors in the sky.
Maybe you just see only one color.

Maybe you just only have one thought that you do not want to have.
Put it in the cloud and let it float away.
It can not hurt you anymore.

You are now feeling very calm, very happy and very very peaceful.
As you sit down in your lovely green field, you realize that nothing can hurt you here and nothing can bother you.
In fact you are feeling very comfortable and very relaxed.
So peaceful and calm just watching the clouds just drift away.
You are breathing gently and calmly, knowing you are very safe here.
Feeling the lovely feelings of happiness and peace.
You are very still and very very relaxed.
You are very happy.

Just sit for a minute and look up at the sky.
It is very blue with only no clouds in the sky.
You noticed all the thoughts that you don't want have disappeared.

All the clouds with your thoughts in them have gone away.
They just floated away.
They can not hurt you anymore.

Now I want you to take a deep breath in through your nose and slowly and gently breathe out through your mouth.
One more time deep breath in.
Slowly and gently breathe out through your mouth.
Now wiggle your fingers and your toes.
Whenever you are ready, slowly and gently open your eyes.

Close your eyes and make yourself comfortable.
Take a deep breath in through your nose and slowly and gently breathe out through your mouth.
Again take a deep breath in through your nose and slowly and gently breathe out through your mouth.
Fantastic!
You are doing really well.
Now imagine that your feet feel all loose and very relaxed.
It is as if they are almost falling asleep.

Can you feel it now?

Imagine all of your body feeling the same way, all loose and relaxed.

You are feeling so relaxed and so very happy.

Now I want you to imagine that you have roots growing out of the soles of your feet.

They look like the roots of a very large and long tree.

Now push those roots deep into the ground.

You can hear them growing deeper and deeper.

You can hear them push their way through the soil.

It tickles.

Can you feel the soil under your feet?

This is called grounding.

This keeps your energy planted into the ground so that you can grow big and strong just like a tree.

Imagine a beautiful white light surrounding your whole body.

This light is so bright that you are shining much brighter than the brightest star.

It does not hurt you to look at this pure white light.

It is protecting you always.

It is as though you have your very own force field around you.

Can you see it?

You are doing amazing.

Now I want you to imagine yourself standing in front of a huge tree.

This tree has deep, deep roots and has branches reaching out in all directions.

You notice this amazing tree has a rope ladder hanging from it.

You look up where it leads, and you see the most beautiful treehouse you have ever seen.

You have always wanted to go and explore your very own treehouse.

Now you have found one just for you.

You have found your secret treehouse.

This is your special place from now on.

You feel so safe and warm.

You feel you can do anything you want now.

Well you can because this is your treehouse.

There are windows, maybe a trapdoor in the floor so you can get down to the ground faster.

You can also have plants in the treehouse.

You can have any kind of plants you want.

Colorful ones, flowers and maybe all of your favorite things.

You can have a swing from the ceiling.

What do you want inside your treehouse?

Think about all the things that make you feel good.

All the things that make you smile.

Maybe it is a favorite toy, or pet or someone special.
Someone you love very very much.
See it in your mind's eye.
Can you see it?
Go ahead and create the inside of your treehouse now.
Make it look just like how you want it.
Anything that makes you happy.
Anytime you feel happy, it gets transported into this treehouse.
Every time you go inside your treehouse you feel so relaxed and so very happy.
This is a place to let go all of your thoughts and all of your worries.
Just let them all go.
They do not matter here anymore.
This is the place to let go of anything that may make you feel sad.
This is a place of happiness just for you.
It is so safe here.
Just be in this treehouse for a few minutes.
Go and explore your very own treehouse.

Do you feel happy now?
Can you feel your heart overloaded with joy?
You are so happy, peaceful and calm.

Everything you have ever wanted is right here with you.

Take a deep breath into your nose and slowly and gently breathe out through your mouth.

You feel very peaceful and very relaxed inside your secret treehouse.

This is a place you go to anytime you want to.

You will always feel calm and peaceful here.

You will be happy to know that your treehouse is always here for you.

In your secret treehouse you are always safe.

You are always loved, and you are always protected.

Take a big deep breath in and imagine yourself walking down the ladder.

Take another deep breath in and slowly and gently bring your attention back into your room.

One more big deep breath in.

Now wiggle your toes, wiggle your fingers, rub your hands together and make them warm.

Whenever you are ready, slowly and gently open your eyes.

You always know that you can come back here anytime you wish.

Relax and sit still and find a place you will not be disturbed.

Maybe you are in your bedroom or your sofa.
Now I want you to take a big deep breath in through your nose and slowly and gently breathe out through your mouth.
Again big deep breath in and slowly and gently breathe out through your mouth.
One more time, big deep breath in and slowly and gently breathe out through your mouth.
Now just relax and let your breathing return to its normal rhythm.

Now I want you to see yourself on your very own private island.
This is a place where only you can go and visit.
It is just for you.
This is your island.
This is your own private place.
This is a peaceful and very, very happy place.

This island is surrounded by the most beautiful and gorgeous blue ocean you have ever seen.
You can see the beach that surrounds the island.
You can hear the sound of the pristine water washing up and down the shore.

The sand is soft and white.
You can feel the warmth of it on your bare feet.
Can you feel it?
Can you feel the sand wiggled in your toes?
Can you hear the waves washing up onto the shore?
Can you smell the salty air of the ocean?
What does that smell like?
In the distance, you can hear seagulls chirping away.

The sun is shining so bright and high in the sky.
There is a gentle breeze blowing through your face.
You lift your head up towards the sun, and you realize you can look at the sun without hurting your eyes.
Can you feel the warmth of the sun on your skin?

Now turn your attention to the beautiful blue ocean.
You watch the sunlight sparkle off the water.
It looks like thousands of diamonds shimmering and sparkle in the light.
They are shining so brightly.
Wow, this ocean is so big, and you realize you are so small.

You start walking towards the sea, feeling the warm hot sun beneath your feet and on your skin.
It feels so warm and so soft.
You walk a few steps into the water and you just stand there.
You feel so relaxed and take a few more steps.
The water is now up to your waist.
You move your hands back and forth in the water.
The water is so clear and you can see the sand beneath your feet.
You put your head into the water and you realize you can breathe!
You're so amazed you are breathing beneath the ocean.
You decide to swim around under the waves.
You feel so delighted and so happy.
The water is very clear and you can see a lot around you.
What can you see?
Can you hear anything?
There are so many fish swimming around you.
They are all shapes, sizes and colors.
Can you recognize any of the fish?
What else can you see?

Now you can hear from far away whales singing.
It's getting closer and closer.
Don't be afraid.
You are safe and so loved.
You are always protected on this island.
You turn around to the deep ocean and see the biggest beautiful face of a whale in front of you!
This whale looks so kind.
You are not afraid at all.
He kind of looks like he is smiling at you, which he is!
You give him a gentle pat on his gigantic head.
Wow, he is so kind and gentle and very curious about you as well.
The whale remains very still and lets you touch him.
What color is the whale?

You can feel the whale's skin with your hand.
You can feel the movement and vibrations coming from his body.
You know that you are not afraid.
He would never ever hurt you.
Can you feel him?
He looks at you and he sees you for who you are.
You look into his beautiful, peaceful big brown eyes.
What do you see?
What do you see in those lovely kind eyes?

What do you feel?
This whale is truly a lovely being.
Can you hear his thoughts?
What is he saying to you?
You can feel the beat of his gentle heart.
You can also see into his beautiful soul.
This soul is so peaceful, so gentle and full of love just for you.

Is there anything you want to say to the whale?
Anything at all?
Whatever you tell him, he will never tell another soul unless you want him to.
He is here to help you.
He is here to heal any worries you may have had.
This beautiful whale will be your new best friend if you would like.
He only wants the best for you.
Go ahead and talk to your new friend.
Talk to him about anything you like.
He is here just for you.

It is now time for the whale to go home.
You wave goodbye and thank him.

He now swims off into the distance.
Thank him for taking the time to be with you, helping you out and listening to you.

Now you can see fish swimming around you.
Remember, anytime you would like to visit this private island and swim, you can.
You can visit this island and the whale again.
Now I want you to take a full deep breath in through your nose and slowly and gently let it out through your mouth.
One last time deep breath in and slowly and gently breathe out through your mouth.
You are feeling very relaxed, very calm and very peaceful.
You feel so happy.
Whenever you are ready, I want you to wiggle your toes and your fingers.
When you are ready, slowly and gently open your eyes.

This is now part of the book just for you.
This part is to help you when you feel a bit worried or stressed.

What I want you to do now is find a nice comfy and cozy position.

Close your eyes and take long slow deep breaths.

When you breathe out, all you are going to do is relax your body.

Awesome, lets begin.

I want you to take a big deep breath in through your nose.

Fill your lungs up.

Now slowly and gently breathe out through your mouth, pushing out all of the air.

Again take another deep breath in through your nose.

Now slowly and gently breathe out through your mouth, pushing out all of the air.

One last time big breath in through your nose.

Now slowly and gently breathe out through your mouth and just relax.

Relax your whole body.

Now I want you to imagine you are standing on a beach.

A beautiful golden beach.

Can you see this beach in your mind?

It could be a beach you have been to before, or you can use an imaginary beach.

Can you see it?

You are now standing on this beautiful golden beach.
The sand is warm beneath your feet.
The sun is warm and lovely on your face.
Look around you.
Walk around and see what this beach has to offer.
You see the huge ocean, and it looks like a deep ocean blue color.
The sunlight sparkles like thousands of diamonds across the water.
Look down at your feet.
In front of them in the Sun is the most glorious shell you have ever seen.
It is so lovely.
It has a golden color to it.
Can you see it?
Pick it up.
The shell feels warm and smooth.
Feel the shell with your fingers.
Can you feel how smooth it is?
Can you feel the tiny ridges on the shell?
This is your magic shell.
You can tell this wonderful and magical shell all of your secrets.
It will keep them for you and it will never tell anyone else.
You can also tell your magic shell any worries or doubts you may have.

You can tell this magical shell about any problems that may be troubling you at the moment.

No matter how big or small they are, your magic shell loves you and cares about you.

Your magic shell only wants you to be happy.

Whenever you have feelings of worry, you can tell your shell about them.

The magical shell will take all these bad and horrid feelings and turn them into good amazing ones.

I want you to see yourself holding this magic shell close to your mouth.

In your mind, silently tell your magic shell whatever you wish, and no one else will ever know what you say.

Only you and your magic shell will know your secrets.

When you say your words, it goes straight into the middle of the shell.

This is so it can take them away for you, so tell your magic shell your worries now.

You do not have to hold back your feelings anymore.

You have given them to your shell.

Your shell will take them away.

Your magic shell has made them disappear.

Just like magic, they are gone.

As you hold your magic shell close, all you feel is happiness and calmness.

You feel so peaceful but really happy.

You feel peaceful from the tip of your tongue to the tip of your nose.

Feel it right now.

Feel how good you feel.

Fell the happy smile on your face.

It is very important for you to know that you can imagine your magic shell whenever you wish.

You can visit your magic shell at anytime you want.

It will always make all those unwanted and bad thoughts and feelings just disappear like magic.

Whenever you wish to feel happy and calm your magic shell will always be there waiting for you in your imagination.

Your very own beautiful golden colored magic shell.

If you want to visit the ocean, you can always look for your own real magic shell.

How will you know it is magic?

You just choose the shell that feels just right for you.

This will be your magic shell, or if you want to, you can use magic stones.

You can also give your magic shell or stone a lovely new name.

You can ask the stone or shell what its name is.

Find a stone outside or on the street or on the playground at school.

You can keep your magic shell or stone under your pillow to take away all the bad dreams.
You can ask your magic shell or stone to always bring you a peaceful night's sleep.
Wow perfect.
Whenever you are ready, I want you to wiggle your toes and wiggle your fingers.
Slowly and gently stretch a little bit.
Whenever you are ready, I want you to just open your eyes.
I want you to find a comfortable place to relax and sit.
I will show you how to do gentle breathing exercises to help you.

Take a deep breath in through your nose and slowly and gently breathe out through your mouth.
Again deep breath in through your nose and slowly and gently breathe out through your mouth.
Very good.
One more time, deep breath in and slowly and gently breathe out through your mouth.
I want you to lift your shoulders right up and touch your ears.
Hold them there for a second and gently put them back down and relax.

One more time, lift your shoulders up to touch your ears and let them drop back down again.

Wow very good.

You are now feeling completely relaxed, warm and tingly.

I want you to imagine a beautiful golden light completely surrounding you.

This light makes you feel warm, safe and so very loved.

Can you see the golden light surrounding your whole body?

I want you to imagine your feet and toes are becoming very heavy.

Gently start to relax them.

It's like a wave that travels up your feet, up your ankles and through the rest of your body.

You are now free to become very heavy, very relaxed and very calm.

I want you to feel this wave as it travels up your shins, your calves and up your knees.

It travels up to the tops of your legs.

You can feel them becoming heavier and heavier.

You feel more peaceful, calm and relaxed.

You feel this wave travel up your whole body.

It travels over your shoulders into your arms and passes down your arms into your elbows into your forearms then hands.

This wave touches you everywhere.
You feel warm and safe and all tingly.
You can feel this beautiful wave as it travels through your wrists and into your hands.
You are feeling so heavy snow, so peaceful, so calm and so relaxed.
You feel the wave as it travels up the back of your neck over to the top of your head.
It tingles and travels down your face.
It becomes very heavy, calm and peaceful.
Your eyes are starting to feel heavy now.
Your ears feel heavy.
Your nose and lips feel heavy.
Even your checks and tongue feel very very heavy now.
You feel so peaceful, so calm, and so relaxed.
Remember that you are always safe, loved and protected.
Always.

You feel so heavy now that your body is not able to move.
But that is okay.
You don't need to move.
You just need to sit peacefully and calmly.
Just rest now.

I want you to see yourself walking down a long hallway with a beautiful tiled floor.
This hallway is lit by gentle beautiful candles on either side of you.
Can you see the shadows of the flames as you walk along?
It is so comforting to you.
You watch them bounce off the walls and feel very peaceful here.
You become excited to see where this hallway will lead.
Where will you go?
At the end of this long hallway, you notice a beautiful curved oak door with a very large doorknob.
You reach out and turn the handle gently and you push the door open.
Wow! Amazing!
You have just entered your very own private garden.
It has big walls all around it and you know that this is your safe place.
This is a place where only you can go.
There is a path ahead of you and you step onto it.
You hear the crunch of the gravel and stones beneath your feet.
On either side of the path, you can see and smell the most colorful and beautiful flowers you have ever seen.

You are now feeling so calm, so warm, so peaceful and so tingly.

You look around and you notice there are walls protecting you and your garden.

They are very old and in some areas are a little worn out.

You listen carefully and you can find that these walls can tell you a story.

Hear it.

Can you hear the stories?

Look around your lovely garden for a few moments and just explore.

You hear something in the distance.

You are not quite sure what it is.

Listen.

Can you hear it?

You realize it is the sound of water.

You follow this sound and look into the center of the garden.

You notice a very old stone well which has vines growing all around the bottom of the well.

The gentle sounds of water becomes louder and louder as you approach closer.

You can see the crystal clear water at the bottom of the well.

It almost looks as blue as the sky.
You look down, and you notice a small sign next to the beautiful old well.
You bend down to read what it says.
It says, "Welcome To The Wishing Well."
Wow! This is a wishing well!
You have to throw a coin in.
You reach into your pocket and grab a coin.
You hold it in your hand and you can feel the weight of this coin.
It is quite heavy and very smooth.
You turn it over in your hand.
If you toss the coin into the water, your wish will be granted.
Do you know what you want to wish for?
Have you decided yet?
Are you sure this is what you really want?
It is now time to toss the coin into the wishing well.
As you do you say the words of the wish.
What is it would you like to say?
Say it now.
You toss the coin and now it is done.
You thank the wishing well for the kindness it has shared.
Now it's time to come back to your bedroom.
You always know that you can come back here to your beautiful garden to visit your wishing well whenever you would like to.

You can come back whenever the time feels right.

I now want you to take a big deep breath in through your nose and slowly and gently breathe out through your mouth.

Again deep breath in through your nose and slowly and gently breathe out through your mouth.

One last time.

Deep breath in and slowly and gently breathe out through your mouth.

Now I want you to wiggle your fingers and your toes.

When you are ready, I want you to slowly and gently relax and sleep.

CHAPTER 4

White Feathered Owl Adventure

Now listen in closely.
Listen very closely.
Remember to gently close your eyes.
I really want you to focus on my voice now.
This is the best way for you to join in on this adventure and imagine.
This is a very special bedtime adventure.
This can only take place in the wonderful and amazing space of your very own mind and dreams.
You will only have the happiest and most fun dreams that you could ever wish for.
Now just make yourself comfortable.
Lie down and stretch out and just snuggle into your bed.
Just relax.

Now take deeper breaths to really relax.
Take in a big slow breath and breathe it all the way out.
Feel the air flowing in and out.
Let go of all your worries now.
Take another big deep breath into your stomach and chest.
Breath all the way out until it flows out like a calm wave.
Notice how much easier it is for you to become more and more relaxed.
Just let yourself go.
Feel yourself settle in and get extra comfy and cozy.
Just feel yourself relaxing more and more.
Awesome job.
You are doing amazing.
Now breath in deeply again and inhaling your best and healthiest breath all the way down into your belly button.
Now let it go all the way out like a gentle wave.
Imagine every breath out from now on is a colorful cloud.
This colorful cloud is releasing all the worries you had and helps you to feel so so good.
Now let your breathing return to normal.
Your breath is no longer something you have to think about now.

With each breath, you feel better and better.
With each breath, you take notice how great each breath feels.
Let yourself sink deeper and deeper into your bed.
Really enjoy the soft bed you are in and all the comfy surfaces around you.
Now here is where your special dream and adventures can begin.

Imagine in your mind's eye and picture you are standing in a happy, friendly and safe forest now.
Here there are so many beautiful and tall trees growing all around you.
There are colorful patches of leaves on the ground and maybe a few twigs and branches here and there.
There are even beautiful blue flowers all springing up from the bushes.
There are also some mushrooms that look interesting as well.
You can see four leave clovers all around you.
You realize that it is nighttime in the quiet forest.
You can see the shiny bright moon shining down its loving light onto the forest.

You can see so many gorgeous twinkling stars floating through the sky.

It's as if they're a thousand diamonds glistening in the night sky.

All around you see the starlight lighting up the forest with a loving and gentle glow.

You feel so loved here, so safe and so special.

Even though it is nighttime you can see very well because of the moon and stars.

It is easy for you to explore around and go anywhere you want to.

The moon shines down, leaving a sparkling trail for you to follow.

Wow this is so magical.

You can see beams of light illuminating the pathway for you to walk and welcoming you to this magical forest.

You decide to follow the light that is shining just for you.

It leads you through the lovely peaceful forest.

You begin to follow the magical light path.

You are feeling so cozy and so warm.

You feel so protected by the moonlight and you feel so free.

You want to explore the forest, and you realize you are the only person here in this peaceful nighttime forest.

As far as you can see, there are no other humans around.

You have this whole forest all to yourself.

Can you hear the chirping of the nighttime crickets?

Can you hear the funny chattering of the squirrels nearby?

You catch a glimpse of some of these squirrels disappearing quickly and scurrying up the tall trees.

For a little while, you are exploring along the forest and feeling so relaxed and good.

It feels great to be walking on your bare feet and can feel the soft grass beneath you.

You can feel the leaves crunching under your toes.

It's as if the ground is gently massaging your feet.

Ahh it feels so nice.

You can smell the pine trees and maple leaves swirling through the forest.

As you breathe in through your nose, these scents just relaxes your body.

It relaxes you even more.

A gentle breeze picks up through the forest.

The leaves are all being picked up and swirled around by the wind.
It sends them into a whirl.

You can't help but notice there is like a swirling tornado.
It is a tiny tornado that is growing, spinning and getting a little bigger.
You look over at the crazy whirlwind, and this tornado is only about a foot tall.
You watch and look at the swirling, spiraling and spinning wind.
It is making leaves fly everywhere, and some are being sucked into this tiny whirlwind.
It even sends some flying at you!
Suddenly this tiny tornado stops spinning and winds down.
Then where the tornado was spinning, you now see a small cute and fluffy owl.
This owl has white feathers and is looking at you in the eyes!
Wow so amazing!
You are so surprised and the white owl says, "Who are you?"
What's your name?

What! Did this owl just speak?

Yes he surely did.

To your surprise you say, well I am just visiting this lovely peaceful forest. Who are you? Whats your name?

The owl tells you that his name is Owen.

He is such a relaxed owl and is just standing there.

You two chat for a little while longer.

He is so funny and interesting.

He is on a little errand for his mother.

You ask him if he needs help because it is always good to be kind and help others in need.

He needs to find something super important for his mom before his bedtime.

She needs it quickly and urgently.

This item will help calm her down at night to help her sleep.

Although I am having a hard time finding it, I have been flying around everywhere like a little tornado.

Let us look together.

He gives you a great big smile and you help the little owl.

You see the path light up by the moonlight again.

He is so relieved that you can help him.

That is very nice and kind of you.

We need to properly explore this nighttime forest.

Use your eyes like an owl.

Owen suddenly flies up to your face and gently rubs his feathers onto your eyes.
When you open them, you suddenly see everything differently.
You can now see like an owl!
You look around and suddenly the forest looks even more lovely.
Everything is so much brighter and so much clearer.
The forest is even more lovely and beautiful now.
You can see all the beautiful plants and trees.
You can see the bright green four-leaf clovers.
You can see those piles of leaves.
Wow, the forest looks so much better.
It's as if you have a new lens and you can see the world in super high definition.
You can even spot tiny insects, crickets and grasshoppers hopping away.
Are you able to now see those squirrels chattering and scurrying about?
You see them run and dart away up the trees.

Wow, it is so magical in this nighttime forest.
It is so magical you can now see like an owl.
Owen looks very happy that you can now see like an owl.

We are looking for something really small.
It is round and it is pale-colored.
It should be white and have a snowy color to it.
It s very small and can even fit into the palm of your hand.
It also has some red spots on it.
Owen can't remember exactly what it is but knows what it looks like.
Just be careful so you don't step on it.
You think hey are we looking for like an egg?
Yes, we are looking for owens sister who is still in her egg and did not hatch yet.
She fell out of the nest and Owen is trying to look for her.
His mom is worried sick now.
Owen also has other siblings at the nest.
Wow an owl egg!
You need to find it quick!
This is very important for you to find the egg.
You both start searching together.
You explore the forest nearby, making sure to look behind every tree, every branch and every rock there is.
Owen says the best thing to do now is to just relax and keep calm under this pressure.
We can do it.

Even though you might be feeling a little of pressure, you are reminded that it is always a good idea to keep your calm.

Relaxing helps you to focus your mind.

You keep searching and then finally, behind the last tree, you see something at the base of it.

It is on top of a patch of four-leaf clovers.

You see something that is white, very smooth, and round.

It's an egg!

You found the egg safely in the four-leaf clover patch.

This must be Owens sister.

You pick up this egg and it is so warm in your hands.

Then the egg starts to wiggle in your hand.

The egg is now moving, wiggling from side to side.

Then a crack suddenly appears.

Owen comes rushing to you.

You and Owen quickly rush to the nest of the whole family.

Owen grabs your hand and you two start flying together.

You can feel your feet lifting off the ground.

You hold onto Owens little claws, and you realize he may be small, but his wings are super strong.

The little Owen easily lifts you and flies you around.
You both fly around in the nighttime air.
It feels so incredible to be lifted up and be flying around in the moonlight.
You feel the fresh rush of the wind around you.
You both fly up higher and higher into the night time sky.
You both climb up and up.
Then Owen starts flying towards a giant oak tree.
This oak tree is enormous and beautiful.
You look around you and you are at the top of all of the other trees in the forest.
You look across the land, and you see so many stars and the clear night sky.
You see the moon glowing and shining.
You feel the winds of the night air pushing you to a soft and gentle landing.
You both land on a very strong oak tree branch.
This branch is very wide and you are standing safely on the enormous tree.

You see all of the other gray and white feathered owls.
They are all excited and surprised to see you.
You are the first human being they have ever met.
You are standing in their warm and cozy nest.

Owen has brought you back into his home.

His home is located safely in the enormous oak tree.

Owen introduces you to his whole wide family.

The other little owls look up to you in amazement.

Owen tells them you were the one who found their little sister.

Owens mother walks over to you and gives you a warm hug and a big huge smile.

She thanks you so much for finding her and made sure her little baby was safe.

The egg starts to crack more now and its just about to hatch.

The little owl pokes its beak and head out of the egg.

The whole owl family huddles around happily.

Now the little owl breaks out of the entire shell, and the family is all smiling around laughing and cheering.

You feel so special and so happy you get to experience this moment with them.

You also feel so warm inside.

The egg is being held in your hand as little Opal is flapping her wings about.

She just hatched, but she already knows how to fly.

She is just flying and circling around your head.

She playfully starts poking at your head and bites your hair.

Haha this is funny and she just tickles you.

After a few moments of her flying around your head, she just gently lands on your shoulder.

Wow she really loves you says the mama owl.

She already knows you are an owl friend.

You should stay and join us.

It was such a long day and we were about to go to bed.

We have an extra big and cozy bed in our branch just for you.

Owens now hops over to you and gives you a pat on the back and welcomes you.

Wow this feels extra special.

Maybe Owen can teach you how to fly next time.

Wouldn't that be amazing?

That would be so special.

All the owls are beginning to yawn.

Everyone is staring at you.

Everyone feels extra sleepy.

Even little Opal needs some rest and sleep.

She used so much of her energy already just to break out of that egg.

You are starting to feel like it is time for you to rest.

Owen shows you to your extra soft and comfy owl bed.

This bed is made out of the softest four-leaf clovers from the forest below.

It also is made out of owl feathers that are so soft, snuggly, and warm to the touch.

You sit down and then lie down completely onto this soft clover feather bed.

You feel so incredibly safe, well protected and secure on this massive giant oak tree.

Owl only makes their nests on the best, sturdiest and safest trees.

You are ready now to just dream and drift away into a good nights sleep.

The shining and twinkling moon light continues to sparkle and glow all around you.

When you wake up tomorrow you know that you will feel so good.

When you wake up you will have returned in your own fluffy and comfortable bed in your home.

You will be taking all the happy dreams and loving memories of your new owl friends.

You will have all the memories of your fun times exploring the forest and helping them out while having so much fun with them.

You know that you are always welcome back here at any time.

You are welcome to have more adventures with Owen and all of his family in the sleepy nighttime forest.

Right now, you are just tucking and nestling yourself inside the soft, comfy and feathered bed.
You are feeling sleepy in their warm and cozy nest.
Very soon you will be falling asleep, just drifting and dreaming away.
You will be floating through your happy dreams.
You will sleep so well.
I hope you enjoy your relaxing and happiest of dreams now.

CHAPTER 5

The Frog and His Magic Drums

Find yourself a nice comfortable place to sit and relax.
Snuggle yourself all up in your bed.
Allow your eyes to gently close and just focus on your breathing.
Take a deep breath in and then slowly and gently breathe out.
Again deep breath in then slowly and gently breathe out.
One more time deep breath in and slowly and gently breathe out and just relax.
Now imagine yourself surrounded by a beautiful white light.
A light so pure and so bright.
This is a light of protection and peace.

Breathe in this white light.

Feel it as it enters your body completely, making you feel warm and safe.

Now you find yourself standing in the most beautiful enchanted garden that you've ever seen.

The sun is shining brightly and it's a very clear day.

You feel very calm, very relaxed and very very peaceful.

You can hear the birds singing to each other and you can feel the lovely gentle breeze on your face.

It is blowing through your hair.

As you walk along this very special garden path, you see that there are flowers growing everywhere.

There are so many of them in so many different colors.

Some flowers are really tall and some of them are very very tiny.

You look ahead of you and you see that the path you are on has two other paths branching off it, and you wonder where it will all go.

It's up to you now to decide which path you take.

Will you carry on straight ahead, or will you go off to the right?

Maybe you want to take the path to the left.

You decide the path and you have chosen the right path for you.

As you walk along this path, you hear beautiful melodic sounds in the distance.

It's faint but you can still hear it.
It sounds so enchanting and so magical.
It makes you feel very happy when you hear it.
You follow this sound.

You reach a giant red toadstool.
It is so huge!
It even has a porch wrapped around it!
It has big windows all painted white.
It has beautiful and nice curtains.
It has a big white door in the shape of an archway.
It is a very fancy toadstool.
You see that the door is wide open, and you wonder who lives in there.
The beautiful sound is calling you.

You walk around the porch to the back of the huge toadstool.
And that's when you see him sitting there playing on his drums.
What you see is a frog.
A beautiful frog and he is just sitting there playing his drum set.

He is so engrossed in his music, and he has not noticed you yet.

You notice he has an earring on his left ear and a green bandana on his head.

He has lots of colorful beads around his neck hanging down from the front of his very bright and colorful shirt.

He even has slippers on his feet, and you can see his hairy toes.

He kind of looks like a hippy frog.

Next to him, you see two beautiful peppermint candles burning brightly.

The flames look like they are dancing to the sound of the drums.

You also see lots of really huge crystals all gathered around him and all over his porch and toadstool.

There are crystals everywhere.

He even has a large sparkling quartz crystal hanging on a silver thread above his head.

The sunlight is bouncing off of this crystal producing rainbows everywhere you look.

This is such a magical and enchanting place.

You can see very large sunflowers all over the porch too.

They look like they are also dancing to the sound of the drums.

They are swaying gently to the rhythm.

It looks like they are having fun too.

You decide to sit down and watch him play and just listen.
You can feel the vibrations.
It is like little tingles of happiness all over your body.
The music is so beautiful.
As you watch, it's like your own personal concert.
It makes you feel very special, so for a few moments, just listen to the magical drums' beautiful sounds.
Feel the happiness run through your whole body.
You can even dance like the flowers.
Can you feel it?

When the drum's sounds slowly stop, you open your eyes, and you realize that the frog is looking at you with a beautiful smile on his face.
You can see now that he has sparkling friendly blue eyes.
The frog says he is not used to having an audience, but he is still thrilled about it.
He says thank you for listening to him play.
He is delighted you enjoyed his music.

He asks you if you would to join him on his little stage which is really his porch with steps leading up to it.

You say you would love to.

The frog explains that this is not just any drum, but it can play melodies, and it makes you really feel the music too, as if you are apart of it.

If you really feel what you are playing and play the notes in a certain order, it can transport you to different lands.

It is like dialing a phone number but with musical notes.

You really have to feel the music.

You have to breathe the music and become the music.

The frog asks if you would like to try it yourself.

Well, of course you would, but you tell him that you've never played a drum before and you are not sure if you can.

The frog just tells you to feel the music.

The magic drum is not about technique.

It is about what you feel inside.

It is about opening your heart.

The frog gives you the magical drumsticks.

You take a big deep breath and close your eyes.

You begin to play even now with your eyes closed.

You just feel where the sticks should go and you start striking the magic drum with the drumsticks.

You feel the music with all your heart.
You become lost in the music.
This is a place where time doesn't exist.
It is just you and the music.

You feel yourself entering what appears to be a tunnel of light and sound.
You can see colors you have never seen before in this tunnel.
You hear sounds you have never heard before.
Wow-what an amazing place.
Feel the joy.
Feel the love.
Spend a few moments here.
Really feel the joy of the music.
Let it fill your heart with feelings of pure joy and pure love.

The frog gently places his hands on your shoulders and brings you back to the present moment.
Your awareness is now back at the toadstool and you realize you had never left this place all this time.
The frog asks what did you see?
What did you hear?

Where did you go?
You tell him about the tunnel of light and sound.
You felt amazing and would really love to do it again.
The frog is amazed that you found the tunnel of light and sound on your very first attempt.
It has never happened before the frog explains to you.
You must be very special indeed.
You feel a little sleepy now so the frog tells you to rest in his hammock.
It is swinging gently on the porch.
You climb up on it and begin to sway from side to side on the very comfy hammock.
It even has very soft pillows to lay your head-on.
The frog tells you that his magic drum has the power to help you to sleep.
The frog begins to play the most amazing and wonderful sounds you have ever heard in your life.
You take a long deep breath in and give out the happiest sigh as you gently begin to fall asleep.
Quietly you hear the beautiful frog say that you can come back and visit him anytime you want.
You drift into a gentle sleep and peaceful sleep.
When you wake up in the morning, you will be in your very own bed and you will feel wonderful.

CHAPTER 6

Sam The Pirate Fish

Find a nice comfortable place to sit and make yourself all cozy in your bed.
Just close your eyes.
Take a deep breath in and then slowly and gently beath out.
Again, deep breath in and slowly and gently let that breath out.
One more time, deep breath in and slowly and gently breath out and just relax.
Stay calm and focused.
Just feel your breathing.
Feel your breath.
Feel your chest as it rises and falls and just relax.
Now imagine you are walking through a beautiful lush green meadow.

It is a beautiful sunny day and the sun is sitting high up in the sky.
You can see lots of fluffy white clouds just gently floating past.
As you continue to walk, you have a look around you.
You notice the most amazing flowers.
They are very pretty and have the most wonderful colors.
Can you tell what kind of flowers they are?
Do you recognize any of them?
Pick one up if you want to.

You feel a little excited with the scents of all these flowers.
The scent makes you very happy indeed.
It is like you're breathing in pure love and happiness.
It is so beautiful.
You continue to walk through your lush green meadow.
You notice that there are tall trees in the distance.
They are very big.
You can also feel the long grass tickling your feet and legs as you walk.
You can hear the birds singing as they fly over you.
You can even hear the flapping of their wings.

Wow! It is so nice here.

You hear the sound of splashing water.
You wonder where it's coming from so you walk towards the sound.
It sounds like it's coming from behind the trees.
You come closer and as you come through the trees, you see a lovely stream.
The sound of splashing is louder now but it is such a peaceful sound.
It is also a very exciting sound too.
You stand beside the stream and watch the water as it tumbles gently over the small rocks.
You watch as it twists and turns as the water tries to go around and over the rocks.
You think it is so cool.
You can even see your own reflection in the water too.
You go in for a closer look, and you see that you have a very beautiful face.
You look at your face and at your reflection.
You can see the beauty and kindness that is inside of you.
It is shining out very brightly because you are a very good and kind person.

This is what other people see when they look at you.
Wow how wonderful you are.

You decide to sit down with your back against a tree.
You let your feet and your legs just dangle in the water.
It feels so cool and refreshing.
You keep watching as the water goes around your legs trying to get past them.
As you sit there, your mind begins to just drift along too.
You find your thoughts are just slipping away.
Just for a moment, allow the gentleness of the water wash all of your unwanted thoughts away.
Just relax for a bit and feel the water on your legs and feet.
Feel the sunshine on your face.
Really feel how good this feels.

Now doesn't that feel nice just sitting here with nowhere to go and nowhere to be?
Just having gentle thoughts.
Suddenly you hear lots of splishy splashy sounds and you wonder what on earth it could be.

You look back at the lazy stream and you are astonished at what you see.

Standing upright in the water is a very brightly colored fish.

It is a deep red color with lots of orange spots on him.

But what is really interesting he is wearing a red pirate hat.

He even has an eye patch like a pirate too.

How strange?

He stares at you and you are a little shocked.

You have never seen a pirate fish before.

Suddenly he speaks and your mouth drops open.

It is a fish that can talk!

He asks what you are and why you are so big.

He tells you his name is Sam and he is a pirate.

He is not really a pirate, but he just likes to think he is.

You tell him who you are, and Sam tells you all about his adventures as a pirate.

Then all of a sudden, he stops and just falls asleep.

The one eye that is not covered by the eye patch is closed.

Then he starts to snore.

Oh my gosh!

Sam is really asleep!

You say wake up Sam wake up.

Sam opens his eye and says oops.
He says sorry I did fall asleep.
I like sleeping a lot.
Sam continues to tell you about his life as a pirate.
For a few moments, you have a chat with him.
Let him tell you what it is like to be a pirate.
Listen to where he goes on his adventures.
Maybe he went to visit other pirates or maybe he and his friends all play at being pirates.
Maybe he might even take you on his adventures.
Now that would be nice right?
Hopefully he won't fall asleep this time.

Where did you go with Sam?
What did you see?
Did you have fun?

Now that Sam has stopped speaking, he falls asleep again.
His eyes are closed again.
He gently starts to snore.
Oh dear poor Sam.
You wonder if you should wake him up or not.
You decide not to as he must be very tired.

A fish gently swims up to Sam and speaks and says not to worry he does this all the time.

We will take care of him.

He very gently lifts Sam up and takes him home.

One of the fishes shouts back to you and says that you are very welcome indeed if you want to come back again.

You say oh yes please!

You wave at the fish goodbye as they gently take Sam home.

You now turn back to the tree and you notice a waterbed next to it.

You didn't see it there before but hey there it is.

You decide to climb on it and rest your body.

You can't stop thinking about Sam the talking fish.

You found it quite funny that he really was a talking fish.

Oh my!

You decide to close your eyes now and rest for a little bit.

You think wow this waterbed is very comfy.

You feel weightless.

It is almost as if you are lying on air or a bit wobbly you feel the bed molding itself around your body as you gently float and wobble a little bit more.

You think this must be what it feels like to lie down on a very big wobbly plate of jello.

You feel so peaceful lying here.
You feel so safe and you feel that the whole world loves you.
The whole world does love you.
You start to feel sleepy now.
You realize that you really do love everybody and that all people are so very very special.
This makes you smile.
You settle yourself down and you relax even further.
You think oh this is the life.
Just being here in this lovely place on this really comfy water bed.
Making new friends named Sam.
You take a big deep breath in and slowly and gently you breathe it out.
Like a great big sigh of happiness.
You feel so happy and relaxed.
You take another deep breath in and then slowly breathe it out.
You feel so sleepy now.
Take another deep breath in and slowly let out the biggest deepest happiest sigh you have ever done.
Even though your eyes are closed, they feel so tired.
Each time you breathe in, you take in all the good thoughts and positive feelings.
Each time you breathe out, you let out all of your unwanted thoughts and watch them drift and float away.

You lie there thinking about your new friend Sam the fish.

You drift into the most wonderful sleep feeling so happy, so safe and so loved.

Goodnight.

CHAPTER 7

Chakra Meditation

Close your eyes now and make sure you are in a very comfortable position.

Enjoy this part of the book as the perfect chakra meditation for kids right before bedtime for an amazing and blissful night's sleep.

You can also use this part of the book to deeply relax at anytime of the day.

Now I want you to imagine there is a powerful energy flowing through your whole body.

This amazing energy is the life force within you.

Your life energy is always glowing inside of yous and shines all around you.

Can you feel it?

Your energy is flowing perfectly between all the different areas of your body.
These areas are called chakras.
When we focus our mind on our chakras, we can grow and flow our energy very powerfully.
We can keep our mind, body and spirit clean happy and healthy.
Your chakras actually shine with every color of the rainbow.
Imagine now a perfect rainbow beaming across the sky and shining right onto you.
Can you see it?

The seven colors of the rainbow are the same seven colors of your chakras.
This energy in you is just like a rainbow.
Wow this is really amazing!
You may think of your chakras now as glowing balls of colorful light energy.
They are all connected to each other and your energy flows between them like a stream of water trickling along a river.
Right now, just meditate on your chakras now.
Just focus your mind on these energy points in your body.

Let's begin at the first chakra.
This is called the base chakra which is at the bottom of your spine.
This chakra point is red.
Imagine a red ball of light glowing here and shining within you at the base of your spine.

You may now imagine a red vortex of light swirling around inside you always keeping you grounded.
Breathe in deeply and out fully now as you are focusing on your base chakra.
You feel supported and safe.
The ground will hold you.
You feel trust and safety.
You are always protected by the divine energy of the universe.
In your mind, you say this incantation to yourself.
I am safe.
I am safe.
I am safe.

Let's now move on to the second chakra which is the sacral chakra.
The sacral chakra is located under our belly button.

This chakra is orange colored.
This area glows with orange light.
Imagine this orange vortex of energy swirling around and shining out of you.
This chakra point is where your creativity flows and your confidence glows.
From this chakra point, breathe in deeply and out fully now.
You are feeling so confident.
You are feeling so inspired and creative.
In your mind, you say this incantation to yourself.
I am always creative.
I am always creative.
I am always creative.

Now focus your energy on your body up to the next area where your stomach is located.
This chakra point is the solar plexus chakra is located where our stomach is.
This chakra point is yellow colored.
Your solar plexus chakra shines with yellow light.
Imagine an orb of yellow energy spinning beautifully in your belly.
Breathe in deeply and out fully as you focus on this area.

As this yellow light spins, it helps you listen to your gut feelings.
It keeps you so healthy.
You feel you can trust your intuition.
You listen to the feelings in your belly.
You feel your sense of power growing.
In your mind, you say this incantation to yourself.
I am powerful.
I am powerful.
I am powerful.

Let's now move upwards to the heart chakra.
The heart chakra is located right in the middle of your chest where your heart is located.
This chakra point is green colored.
This chakra point glows with a lovely green ball of light shining out to the world from within you.
You can feel and see this swirling green energy in your heart.
Breath in deeply and out fully.
Just focus on this area.
You can feel your heart chakra increasing your loving and kindness towards yourself and others.
You feel your loving connections to other people
You feel so much love for all living things.

In your mind, you say this incantation for yourself.
I am loving.
I am loving.
I am loving.

Now let's move up to your throat chakra.
This chakra point is blue colored and located in your throat and neck.
This chakra glows with blue light energy.
This blue colored ball of divine light twirls around and around in perfect harmony.
Breath in deeply and out fully.
Focus on this area.
You can feel that the throat chakra is your communication center.
You feel you can easily express yourself.
You feel so at ease in communicating well with others.
You feel how good it is to speak your truth and to be yourself.
In your mind, you say this incantation to yourself.
I am truthful.
I am truthful.
I am truthful.

Now let's move your focus now to your third eye chakra located right between your eyes in the middle space of your head.

This very special chakra point glows with an indigo color.

Indigo is the color of blueberries.

Imagine this light energy swirling perfectly in your mind.

Breath in deeply and out fully now and just focus on this area.

You feel your thoughts are very wise.

You feel your dreams are sacred.

You feel and think with your spirit.

With your third eye, you see the energy of all living things.

In your mind, you say this incantation to yourself.

I am wise.

I am wise.

I am wise.

Now move your focus to just above the very top of your head.

This is the highest chakra of your body and is called the crown chakra.

This chakra sparkles and shines with a violet purple light.

Imagine a crown balancing on the top of your head made out of this violet divine light energy.

Now imagine this violet light energy is swirling around like a ball of pure peace.

Breathe in deeply and out fully.

Focus on this sacred area just above your head.

You feel a higher sense of being alive.

You feel connected to all that is.

You feel that you are apart of everything in this world and everything is apart of you.

You feel your imagination is free.

Your imagination expands out to the whole universe.

You feel that you are a divine universal energy.

In your mind, you say this incantation to yourself.

I am divine.

I am divine.

I am divine.

Now say thank you to the magnificent universe.

Thank you.

Thank you.

Thank you.

Your seven chakras are now in perfect alignment and harmony.
You are a wonderful rainbow of glowing energy and colors.
Your glorious energy shines perfectly through your mind, body and spirit.
Your energy flows like a lovely stream from the crown chakra all the way down to your base chakra. Then all the way back up from your base chakra to your crown chakra.

You have done a brilliant job through this meditation.
Well done for learning all about your chakra and deepening your connection to the universe.
You are feeling so relaxed and so incredibly peaceful.
It is now time to drift off into a cozy deep peaceful sleep.
I hope you enjoy the most happiest sleep or your most relaxing day.
I hope you have blissful dreams and the most wonderfulest of day dreams.
I am sending and wishing lots of love and light from the whole universe.
Namaste.

CHAPTER 8

Lucid Dreaming Meditation

Let's begin our guided lucid dreaming meditation.
In case if you are wondering what lucid dreaming is, lucid dreaming is the ability to know that you're dreaming while you're dreaming which means once you are conscious you can fly, experience wild fantasies, and more importantly you can even connect to the awareness behind the dream.
Now you know what lucid dreaming is, it's important to keep a dream journal with you every morning right when you wake up and write down everything you can remember.
The more you make this a habit, you will not only remember your dreams, but you will also be able to remember your lucid dreams as well.
This is because we have longer durations of REM sleep towards the end of our overall sleep cycle.

REM sleep is actually when we are dreaming.
Let's now begin the relaxation process.
Allow yourself to get really comfortable.
If you are laying down, feel free now to lay your hands by your sides or on your lap.
Whatever is the most comfortable for you.
Close your eyes and think of your whole body going limp and relaxed.
Imagine the muscles in your scalp and forehead growing very comfortable and relaxed.
You will find as you think about these muscles relaxing, they will do as you say.
As the muscles in your forehead relax you may notice slight tension around the eyebrows.
Concentrate on the eyebrows and all around your eyes and this tension will fade away.
Now feel the tiny muscles of the eyelids relax.
Feel the relaxation now move deeply inside your eyes and deepen back in the eyes.
Let all of your facial muscles relax.
Relax your cheekbone, cheeks, jaw, chin and lips of your mouth.
As your mouth muscles relax, you will find that your mouth automatically becomes not too moist, not too dry but just moist enough to keep you perfectly comfortable.

Now feel the relaxation spread deep into the back of your throat, deep in the back of your head and neck.
Feel the relaxation deep into the neck and shoulders.
Let your arms relax.
Relax the upper arm.
Concentrate on the forearms and feel the relaxation.
Relax all the muscles between the elbows and the wrist.
Just feel the relaxation spread across the top of your hands and deep into the hands.
Feel the relaxation deep into your palms.
Let your fingers relax all the way down to your fingertips.
As your fingers relax, you may or not experience a slight tingling sensation in your fingers.
If you do, then you will notice it to be a very pleasant sensation.
It's a very pleasant tingling in your fingers.
Now bring your attention back again to the relaxed muscles of your neck and shoulders.
Let the relaxation flow into the chest and lungs.
Your breathing is now easy and gentle.
You feel yourself relaxing more and more with each gentle and easy breath.

You relax more and more with each sound of my voice.

All of the outside sounds are unimportant.

Only the sound of my voice is important right now.

Let the relaxation spread to the top of your back and feel it move gently down your back to the small curvature in your spine.

Let all of the muscles of the body go to sleep and in a sense while remaining perfectly conscious and aware.

Concentrating now on the relaxation spreading deep into the sides of your abdomen.

Let all of the muscles in your stomach relax deep into the stomach.

Let all of the muscles of the stomach and hips relax.

Now let your legs relax and feel this relaxation spreading to your thighs and knees and to your calves of the legs.

Relax all the way down to the ankles and now let the feet relax.

Relax the heels of your feet, the undersides of your feet, the tops of your feet and finally your toes.

Relax.

It feels so good to relax and let go of all the tension and care.

Now in a moment, I will begin to countdown.

With each descending number, your level of relaxation will double.

Allow this relaxation to happen now.
Five.
Sink deeper and deeper down.
Four.
Feel so calm so peaceful and so relaxed.
Three.
Let go.
It feels so good to just let go.
Two.
Getting closer now.
One.
Now you are peacefully and comfortably relaxed.
Now that you have relaxed, take a moment to enjoy this peaceful and private place within.
Just allow the tranquility to engulf your entire being.
Now in a moment, we are going to embark on your journey into the magical world of lucid dreams.
In fact, it will be quite easy once you understand that all it involves is just learning to communicate with your unconscious mind.
This can be done through affirmations and visualizations just like this audiobook.
Now once you begin, you dream that the new world opens up to you.
One that's free of the laws of physics and one that's free of judgments.
Anything is possible in this new wonderful world of lucid dreams.

Now I would like you to imagine yourself walking along a path in the forest and allow yourself to see and sense your surroundings around you.

Allow yourself to notice the trees, the leaves, and the grass.

Allow yourself to hear the birds and just pay attention to the beautiful sounds resonating from your surroundings.

As you continue down this path, you begin to see big floating bubbles intertwined between the tress and this forest's surroundings.

These bubbles appear to have 3d images that are somewhat transparent but noticeable.

As you continue walking down this path, you realize that these 3d images are actually dreams you have had from the past.

These are only dreams that have some sort of importance to you.

As you continue to walk down this path, you see a sign that says this is the Rainforest of Dreams.

The sign also says if you continue down this path, you will enter the world of dreams.

As you get closer, you begin to realize that these images are not really bubbles but portals to your dream world.

Allow yourself to look around at these bubbles.

How do you feel about this portal?

Do you want to go through it?

Now for a moment, when you step through this portal, you see you will find yourself and a dream from the past.

This can be any dream you may have had before.

It could be the one from last night or a dream you have not had for a long long time.

When you enter a dream from the past and when you do enter into it, you will notice everything in this dream in colorful and vivid detail.

Now when you are ready, step through this portal.

Now look through your dream eyes.

We are in this dream now.

What do you notice about your surroundings?

Are you indoors or outdoors?

Are there any dreamy figures in your dreamy landscape?

In this dream, are you actually you?

Or perhaps you are someone else.

Now for a moment, I would like you to take a step back from the dream and allow yourself to get recentered.

You can do this by following my voice.

Just take a few moments to do this.

Before we go back and to the dream world.

Amazing.

You are doing great.

Now in your mind's eye, I want you to imagine you are back in your same dream.

This time however, I want you to see yourself recognizing that you are dreaming.

Perhaps something in your dream realized now you are actually dreaming.

Maybe if you are an intermediate lucid dreamer maybe you did a reality check and you realized you were dreaming.

Whatever makes sense to you is perfectly fine.

Amazing.

You are doing great.

Realize you are dreaming.

It is time to set your intention to lucid dream.

Perhaps you want to fly.

If you want where would you go?

Would you like to fly around your city or would you prefer to fly in outer space?

Maybe you want to experience an awesome and wild fantasy or practice a hobby you love.

Whatever it may be it is up to you.

This is your dreamworld.

Anything is possible.

Just remember this dream world is free of judgement.

Feel free and experience whatever it is you would want to experience.

For the next few minutes, visualize yourself becoming aware.
Set your intent on lucid dreaming.
That's amazing, you're doing great.
Now that you set your intent on tonight's lucid dream, let us amplify this intention's power.
Say this following affirmation internally in your mind.
When you do this, you really feel it.
Feel it in your heart's center.
At the same time, be free from the outcome.
You should be free of stress when you do this.
Just search your intent and then let it go.
Now in your mind, repeat after me.
The next time I am dreaming, I will remember her to recognize that I am dreaming.
Amazing.
This affirmation is so powerful that just by saying this affirmation along before going to bed or in the middle of your sleep cycle can actually increase your probabilities of having lucid dreams.
Now let's say this affirmation one more time.
The next time I am dreaming, I will remember to recognize that I am dreaming.
Amazing.
You are doing great.
One more time, I would like you to see yourself in a precious dream.

Once again, become aware and then deciding to achieve your lucid dreaming goal.
Then follow that up again with the affirmation.
The next time I am dreaming, I will recognize that I am dreaming.
Feel free and cycle between these two techniques.
When you wake up in the morning, you will remember all your dreams and lucid dreams with total and complete ease.

CONCLUSION

Thank you so much for listening to *Bedtime Meditations For Kids.*

I hope this book has helped you have lots of wonderful dreams and amazing nights of sleep.

If you ever find yourself stressed out, angry, overwhelmed or sad, you can always refer to this book's teachings and re-listen to it again.

If you enjoyed this book and if it has helped you have a better night's sleep, be sure to leave a thoughtful review on Amazon of how this book has helped you. This is so more kids like you can have amazing sleeps every night!

Thank you again for listening to this book and I wish you all the love, happiness and amazing nights of sleep ahead!

www.ingramcontent.com/pod-product-compliance
Lightning Source LLC
Chambersburg PA
CBHW071957110526
44592CB00012B/1120